Just Breathe

Learning to Love Yourself Well Through Life's Challenges

By

PRISCILLA DIANE COFFEE

Refresh and Refuel Publishing

CONTENTS

Dedication & Acknowledgements   7

Introduction   13

Chapter 1:   Perspective Changes Everything   17

              Who Am I?   24

Chapter 2:   S.L.A.P.P.'s....Stress   29

              The S. L. A. P. P.'s In Life   30

Chapter 3:   S. L. A.P.P.'s....Loss   41

Chapter 4:   S.L. A. P.P.'s....Anxiety   51

Chapter 5:   S.L.A. P.P.'s....Pain & Pressure   69

              Redefine Your Experience   79

              Re-Think Your Story   80

Chapter 6:   **What Story are you telling yourself?**   85

My COVID19 Story   87

Re-Write Your Story   92

Chapter 7:   **Your Healing Begins Within**   101

Love Starts Here   103

Agape...Unconditional Love   104

Phileo...Love Your Neighbor As Yourself   107

Self-Affirmations... Confessions   110

Forgive (Grace & Space)   113

Chapter 8:   **Your Relationships Matter**   117

Relationships   118

Relational Accessibility   119

You Lead   124

Life Enhancing Relationships...   128

Be the Friend You Desire to Have in Your Life   134

Chapter 9:   **Are You Listening To Yourself?**   137

Living in Alignment   138

Your Mind, Will & Emotions   141

Chapter 10:   Self-Care Isn't Selfish   145

You are Worth It   146

Relational Wellness   147

Emotional Wellness   149

Physical Wellness   151

Spiritual Wellness   153

Chapter 11:   Prioritizing Your Wellbeing   161

Loving Yourself Well   162

Developing A Self-Care Plan   163

Enjoy Your Journey   167

Each One Teach One   169

References   171

About the Author   173

DEDICATION & ACKNOWLEDGEMENTS

This book is dedicated to my Amazing and supportive family.

First, to my mommy, Diane Easter, I love you and I miss you more than words could ever express. It's remembering your strength, courage, and love that has gotten me through some of the most difficult moments in my life.

To Malcolm, my oldest son, you have been my strength from the first time I laid eyes on you and your big beautiful brown eyes looked back at me. Your very entrance into this world blessed my life with the joy of experiencing the responsibility of motherhood!

To Krisean, my encourager! You know how to make me laugh! Your smile, joy, and laughter are contagious and have gotten me through the toughest of times.

To Mikaila, my sweet baby girl. You are my joy, my beloved, my beautiful, sweet blessing from the Lord! Your confidence in me is awe-inspiring! I love you!

To Mariah, I love you sooo much! You are my motivator. Your fearlessness, drive, and faith motivate me to push beyond the ordinary.

Last, but most definitely not least, to David, my heartbeat, my sunshine, my inspiration, my day one, my best friend, and the love of my life. If I began to describe who you are to me, I would fill this book but that is for another time. Thank you for always being my greatest supporter. ¡Amo a mi Familia! (I love my family!). You are my joy and my song.

Love Always,

Priscilla Diane Coffee

Keep Living...

You can get through this Stress

You can get through this Loss

You can get through this Anxiety

You can get through this Pressure

You can get through this Pain

Just Breathe...

Take A Deep Breath...

Let's do this together...Okay, here we go!

INTRODUCTION

What does it mean to BREATHE?...

Breathing is a life function. Breathing refreshes us from one breath to the next. I would posit that our breaths refresh us Spiritually and Emotionally as well as Physically. My reason for writing this book is to Encourage, Inspire, and to Empower you through some of the most difficult times that you may face in life to Just Breathe.

When we breathe, we inhale, and we exhale...

I believe that what we inhale has the power to refresh us or to deplete us.

To Inhale is to Inspire: **Inspire means** to excite, encourage, or breathe life into. **Inspire** comes from the Latin word that **means** to inflame or to blow into. When you **inspire** something, it is as if you are blowing air over a low flame to make it grow.

That's powerful!

Then the LORD God formed the man from the dust of the ground. He breathed the breath of life into the man's nostrils, and the man became a living person.

Gen 2:7

The Breath of God is Healing, Restorative, and Igniting. He is our Creator and He loves us deeply. So, when we inhale His breath, our hearts, our minds, our bodies, and our spirits respond.

To Exhale is to breathe out. What's amazing about this is that when we inhale our bodies take the oxygen that we need into our blood cells and the waste gas that is left over (carbon dioxide) after our bodies process what we inhale is exhaled or breathed out.

In this, I see the beautiful way that God designed us to process what is necessary for a healthy life while also getting rid of toxic, harmful things.

To Breathe is to Respire: **Respire means** to inhale and exhale successively. It also means to recover hope, courage, or strength after a time of difficulty.

This book is a breath of fresh air to the heart and the soul of the person who is living life every day showing up for the people and the things that they care most about while leaving themselves unheard and uncared for. Yes. I'm talking about you. Listen, I'm not saying that neglecting to care for yourself has been intentional, but I am saying that this book was written just for you. It's your time. Journeying through the pages of this book is your time and your space to show yourself some love, kindness, and grace. This is your place of self-discovery. This is your time to finally listen to your heart to find out what it is that you really need and begin caring for the broken, the hurting, the mentally, emotionally, and physically exhausted spaces inside of you. It's your time to begin healing. You're not alone. I'm right here with you. Thank you for taking the time with me to stop for a few moments and Just Breathe.

Chapter One:

PERSPECTIVE CHANGES EVERYTHING

Who or what has **inspired** your
thoughts of who you are today?

You're okay...It's gonna be okay...

.... And her lungs filled with oxygen as she slowly and deeply drew in the crisp clean air that gave her a sense of peace, comfort, and reassurance that it was all gonna be okay and she quietly whispered, "It's Okay, Just Breathe...You're Okay, it's gonna be Okay."

I remember sitting on my couch stressed out and crying, rubbing my hair and saying to myself over and over again. "It's okay, just breathe...you're okay, it's gonna be okay." I was a single mother living in my apartment with my 3-year-old son. I learned these words of comfort from my mother when I was a little girl.

My mother died when I was incredibly young, but these words stuck with me and brought me comfort when I needed it most. Most of my family lived miles and miles away, and although it would be nice to have them near, it was the comfort of my mother that I missed the most as she would say these words to me.

That moment on the couch was a moment in my life when I wished that she was with me just as she was when I was a little girl. I remembered like it was yesterday how she would rub my back when I was sick with a tummy ache and throwing up in the middle of the night. I hated to throw up...and still do. It was so scary as I gasped for breath every chance I could between throwing up. I remembered that my mom would stay with me and rub my back ever so gently. She would place cold towels on my forehead and say to me "It's okay, you're okay" and I knew that I was gonna be okay.

As I grew up, I found myself saying those words to comfort and soothe myself during difficult times.

There are a lot of people struggling through life unable to find any peace or comfort. Life is beautiful but can also be very hard at times. I know that you know this. I know that you've felt like this at one point or another. Most times, when we feel this way, we begin to search for a way to ease our suffering even if just temporarily. Some of us run to comfort food, friends, and TV. shows or anything to distract us for the moment and that's okay temporarily. It helps. What doesn't help is when we find unhealthy ways to cope with what we're facing like substances, reckless behavior, or unhealthy relationships; trying anything that works for the moment to soothe the pain. It breaks my heart that so many people struggle to find healthy ways to work through life's challenges.

Listen. No one enjoys pain. Many of us deal with self-doubt, insecurities, fear, shame, low self-worth, anxiety, depression, stress, distress, heartbreak, heartache, and so many more painful things. There are so many people searching for ways to deal with emotional pain. It is a very tough thing to acknowledge but the way that many of us deal with it is by masking the pain with something else that will hurt us in the extremely near future. Our logic for operating this way is that it works. For now, at least. It feels better now. We try our best not to think about what it does to us in the long run. As long as it brings immediate relief to us now. The problem with this logic is that if we plan to keep living and for things to be different, we have to address these things from a perspective that considers our long-term emotional health and well-being.

Earlier I mentioned breathing. It may seem like such a minor thing, but I think that there is so much more to breathing than we realize. We are going to explore breathing throughout this book because I believe that there are some vital truths to unveil in this simple yet essential function of living.

Since we know breathing in its simplest form is inhaling and exhaling, just breathing in and out. I wonder if you've ever considered how amazing it is that we do this so automatically. As long as we are alive, we breathe without even thinking about or second-guessing the breaths that we take. This is a fascinating thought. Studies show that most adults take an average of 12-20 resting breaths per minute, which in turn add up to 720-1,200 breaths per hour and 17,280-28,800 breaths per day. Just imagine that we do all of this without a second thought.

Well, when we consider this then we must be aware that what we inhale or breathe in affects our body either positively or negatively. What we inhale will either be life-giving and helpful or toxic and detrimental to our health and well-being. For instance, an environment that is negative, draining, and threatening to one's mental health and well-being is a toxic environment. Inhaling the toxicity of negativity, lies, gossip, slander, and hate just to name a few, not only hinders us but corrupts, tears down, and annihilates our mental health and wellbeing.

On the other hand, an environment that fosters peace, trust, joy, faith, hope, encouragement, and love nurtures, builds up, fortifies, and influences our mental and emotional health to thrive and flourish.

With this thought process in mind, we can surely see how what we inhale is going to affect our lives now, as well as in the future. I believe that the Bible makes a strong case for this line of thinking where the scriptures say...

"And He breathed the breath of life into the man's nostrils, and the man became a living person."

Genesis 2:7

The man existed but as a lump of molded clay until God breathed life into him. Notice that the scripture says that the man BECAME. Whatever you are breathing is shaping you into whoever you are becoming. Every breath that we take is vital to our living and our flourishing. Since this is the case, I believe we ought to take great care to place ourselves in an environment that will not only be life-sustaining but life-giving.

After all, that makes the difference between us merely surviving, gasping for every breath as we struggle through life, and having the ability to live and breathe through life's triumphs as well as through life's storms.

We can in fact enjoy the beautiful life that we have been given although life is full of both trials and triumphs.

Okay, before we move on, let me introduce to you a couple of tools that we will practice together throughout the upcoming chapter. These techniques will prove to be beneficial to you for life.

The first is Deep Breathing...

First, get into a comfortable position. Close your eyes. Breathe in through your nose and fill your tummy with air. Place your hand on your tummy so that you feel it rise as you breathe in. Exhale through your mouth by blowing the air out. You will feel your tummy lower. Take your time and do this slowly three times.

The first time breathe in slowly through your nose feeling your tummy rise... then exhale slowly through your mouth blowing the air out through your lips...feel your tummy lower, roll your shoulders back and down away from your ears and imagine yourself releasing any tension that you're feeling at the completion of each breath.

Next, breathe in slowly through your nose thinking of breathing in peace and calm ... and exhale slowly through your mouth rolling your head around while thinking of blowing out stress and anxiety... Aaaah that feels goooood.

Finally, breathe in slowly through your nose the breath of peace and calm...and exhale slowly through your mouth experiencing totally relaxed head, neck, shoulders, and arms.

You can continue this exercise until you feel totally relaxed.

The second is Grounding...

This technique is going to be immensely helpful for you because we are going to be discussing some things that may be anxiety-arousing. If you have experienced trauma, struggled with nightmares, or remember situations that cause you to feel threatened or unsafe. This will help you to bring yourself into the current moment where you can recognize that you are safe.

We will be utilizing our 5 senses counting down from 5...4... 3... 2...1

Look around the room and name 5 things that you can see and describe them.

Listen carefully and name 4 things that you can hear and describe if they are loud, faint, funny etc...

Touch 3 things within your reach and describe how they feel.

Describe 2 things that you currently smell.

Describe 1 thing that you currently taste. (it could be gum, or coffee or the residue of some good food you ate.)

Now...

Take a deep Breath... and say "It's Okay, I'm okay. I'm safe."

You can take as many of these comforting, and reassuring deep breaths as you would like.

Are you ready? Let's talk a bit about the way that you see yourself and how this impacts your life.

WHO AM I?

Well, when you ask most people who they are they start off by mentioning that they are a mother, father, husband, wife, doctor, teacher, etc... Rarely do you ever hear a person describe themselves from the inside out. When I say that I mean, if all those things were stripped away from us, who would we be? When we discover this, when we unearth this, I believe that we will unlock something inside of ourselves that is freeing. When we detach our value from the way that we show up for other people. I believe that we will begin to see the magnificent person that God created us to be flaws and all.

I have heard people say that we are the sum total of our experiences in life and that we are a product of our environment. I can partly agree with that because our experiences color the lens through which we see life while our environments are often a place where we can flourish and grow or a place that is not conducive for our betterment at all.

I have also heard it said that we are a product of our decisions and not governed by our circumstances. I definitely do believe that we are a product of our decisions but with that being said, we are also always one decision away from changing our circumstances.

What have you heard? Better yet, what do you believe about who you are and why you are the way that you are? What you believe is what matters. Why? Because what you believe shows up in the way that you live your life.

Just know this, as you embark upon this healing journey with me, you're going to learn to challenge unhealthy and unhelpful thoughts that you may have had for a long time. And you are going to begin to see yourself through more loving and gracious eyes. My hope is that you begin to see yourself through the same loving eyes that your loved ones see you through. More importantly, my prayer for you is that you really open your heart to seeing yourself through the loving and compassionate eyes that God sees you with. Trust the process. You have been waiting a long time to begin this healing journey. It's your time.

So, let's begin...

Let's start by taking a deep breath.

Breathe in through your nose slowly...Now exhale through your mouth slowly letting out a sigh of relief...

One more time...

Aaaaaah, that felt good...

Now here we go... Let's get into it!

PRISCILLA DIANE COFFEE

Chapter Two:

S.L.A.P.P.'S
....STRESS

In the midst of the chaos of life, give
yourself permission to slow down
and to give yourself what you need.

THE S. L. A. P. P.'S IN LIFE

Life happens.... Better yet, Life be Lifeing... Have you ever heard that said? I assure you; that life happens to us all. Sometimes things in life can totally blindside us or "knock us off of our square" so to speak. I have had times in my life where I felt like I didn't know which way was up. Difficult times happen to us all. No one is exempt from facing what I call the S. L. A. P. P.'s (Stress, Loss, Anxiety, Pain & Pressure) in life. What we need to know though is that these things happen, but they won't destroy us. They are difficult but not insurmountable. They hurt but we can heal. They may be some of the most difficult things that we have ever faced but they are not the end of the road for us.

Let's take a look at some of these daunting things and explore the opportunity for hope and healing that we have when we learn how to breathe through the S. L. A. P. P.'s that we face in life.

STRESS

It was absolutely appalling to learn that the number one cause of most Doctor visits is due to stress-related illnesses. I'm sure you have felt the weight of daily stressors in your own life. Society's norm is for us to run at such a fast pace that we are constantly trying to get more done in less time. We try to squeeze a dollar out of 15 cents. We try to get as much time as possible out of the 24 hours that the day holds. Have you ever considered that no one person is privileged to have more time in one day than another? We all get the same amount of time each day. So, why is it that we stress ourselves to the max? Why do we overload our "To Do Lists" causing ourselves to live in the false reality that we've created that says that living this way is necessary to be productive? It's not true! Why do we think we can continue this ridiculous race against time?

When living like this it's easy to find ourselves without enough sleep, little to no exercise, living off fast food, and to top it all off, we do all of this with no real fulfillment or meaningful use of our days. We look up and a day has passed, and we get up and do it all over again tomorrow. If we're not careful a week passes by, a month, and even a year and we are still living an unmanageable, stressful life. Something's gotta Give!

When I think about this, my heart cries out...

Teach me to number my days, so that
I may gain a heart of wisdom.

Psalm 90:12

If we go through life racing and chasing after things... one day we will realize that we have gone through life chasing after the stuff with no real value in the long run. I don't know about you, but the thought of having lived life without much meaning at the end of my days shakes me to my core. I desire to live my life to the fullest, doing things that mean something to me and spending time with the people who mean everything to me.

So, I often have to step back and evaluate what is most important to me. I have to assess whether the things that I'm busy with in life are things that are just keeping me busy, or if it is fulfilling purposeful life work. What's important to you? What would give great value to the life that you've lived when you arrive at the end of your days?

Re-evaluating how I spend my days and what I devote my time and efforts to helps me to get rid of unnecessary stress. You know how sometimes we say yes to things and get caught up in stuff that we really don't want or need to be doing that ends up stressing us out? Re-evaluating how you spend your days so that you can remove unnecessary stressors is something that I would recommend that you consider doing from time to time to get yourself back on track to living a life that is full of purpose and meaning.

The race against time is one thing that we stress about but you may be thinking there are so many other things that are stressful in my life like my job, my relationships, my family, my health, my bills, and on, and on, and on. I know that sometimes there is so much going on in our lives that we feel like we are scarcely making it. We feel like we're just functioning enough to keep going. Sometimes we are so stressed that we feel like "If one more thing happens, I'm gonna break". You ever feel like "I'm on a thin thread and any added pressure is gonna just snap this thread that I'm barely hanging on to?" You are not alone. Unfortunately, you are in good company. Way too many of us feel like this far too often. You, my friend, need some breathing room.

Do something for me, right here and right now as you are reading. Stop and take a deep breath.

Inhale slowly...now exhale...

Inhale slowly... now exhale...

one more time, Inhale slowly... now exhale.

You should be feeling a little more relaxed. The tension that you were just feeling should be lessened. I need to tell you something...

You are going to make it

It's a good time to bring up professional support. I support going to therapy. If you feel like you are not emotionally well, it's a wonderful idea to see a therapist. We go to our primary care physicians when we are not feeling well physically and I'm here to tell you that it is just as important to tend to our mental and emotional wellness. I had to throw that in there because the idea that we have to be "crazy" to see a therapist is nonsense. We don't need to wait until we feel like we're broken into a million pieces and can't put ourselves back together again to connect with someone who can support us now.

I also want you to be encouraged if you've ever gone to therapy and didn't quite like it because you didn't connect well with the therapist. Therapists are people and just like you connect to some people better than others the same is true for therapists. It's important that you have a good therapeutic relationship with this person because you are going to be sharing some of the most intimate details of your life with them and you want to feel that you can trust them, and you want to feel supported and helped. If you start seeing someone and you don't feel a good connection, it's more than okay to try another therapist. You are not seeing them for them. You are seeing them for you. This is about your mental and emotional well-being so don't stick around and be committed to a relationship with a therapist that is not working for you. Move on. When you find the right therapist, you will be sooo glad that you have them in your corner.

Listen. You are not alone. You do not have to face what you've been going through all alone. Let's walk through life together, in community with others. Having the support, you need in people who care about you and will walk alongside you while you process and cultivate new hope, gives you strength you don't have on your own.

There is Power in Loving Support.

Open the doors of your life and allow the right relationships to share your burdens. We were never meant to do life alone. People possess a wealth of wisdom and insight. When we open ourselves up to receive the gems that people in our supportive relationships have and want to share with us, we will be blessed because of it. We ought not stand on the sidelines of life suffering, waiting on God's voice to crack the sky to give us something that He has already placed within someone we are connected to. Let the right people in! Let the right people love you! Let the right people walk with you!

You're doing it right now! I'm so happy that you picked up this book and made the decision to be free from the Stress that has been trying to take over your life. I'm honored to be the person who is able to walk with you at this juncture of your life. Taking the time to read this book and apply the things that you learn is going to transform your mental and emotional health. I say that because I believe that *there is Power in Life-Giving Perspective.* When we are able to look at our lives from a different angle, a more positive angle, an angle that shows us that challenges present opportunities for us to grow personally and to solve problems in the world everything changes.

Life-Giving Perspective stimulates and develops your vision to see opportunities for positive change that you can harness to create favorable solutions for the difficult things that you are facing. Let me say that again,

> *Life-Giving Perspective, stimulates your mind to envision and create life-changing solutions to your problems!*

So, changing your perspective has the power to change everything!

Learn to take a firm grip on what creates stress inside of you instead of allowing It to grip You. When you practice becoming more self-aware you gain the ability to take notice of distressing things, address them head-on, and create peace where there would've been turmoil.

Let's do some self-inventory. Get your notebook and write down the answers to these questions.

Ask yourself.

- What is creating stress within me?
- What are the current sources of stress in my life?

Ask yourself.

- What does peace mean to me?
- What activities or practices bring me a sense of calm?
- What positive changes can I make in my life to promote peace and reduce stress?

Then, ask yourself this miracle question. If when I woke up in the morning, everything was perfectly peaceful, and all my stress was gone.

- How would I know?

- What would things look like?

- What would be different?

- What would I be doing?

- What would I be feeling?

- Who would I be around?

After you answer those questions, do this. Consider what you listed things would look like if things were different, and then ask yourself...

- Can I implement some of these things in my life right now so that I can experience more peace and joy?

The thing is... most of the things that people list when they do this exercise are simple things that are accessible, and that they can do to enjoy life more right now. The problem is that we've allowed life's stressors to get so much in the way that accessing this peace seems far away and unattainable. I'm here to remind you that you can enjoy these things now and experience the PEACE that comes with it.

PEACE IS POSSIBLE

You CAN do this! You've been so overwhelmed for so long that these things seem out of reach but trust me. It's time to take your peace off the shelf. You can start by exploring new ways to experience the simple things in a way that breathes new life and joy into your days.

Here are a few ideas...

1. **Nature:** Take a mindful nature walk, pay attention to the details, and observe the beauty of God's creation around you.

2. **Cooking:** Experiment with new recipes or try your hand at cooking a favorite dish from scratch.

3. **Reading:** Explore different genres or authors you haven't tried before.

4. **Photography:** Take pictures from unique angles, experiment with lighting, or focus on capturing everyday objects in a creative way.

5. **Art:** Try painting, drawing, or any other form of creative expression, even if you're not an artist. You might surprise yourself.

6. **Music:** Learn to play a new instrument or listen to genres of music you're not familiar with.

7. **Exercise:** Try a new fitness routine or outdoor activity to keep things interesting and refreshing. Try yoga outside on the grass.

8. **Travel:** If you can, explore new places within your local area or become a tourist in your own city.

9. **Meditation:** Explore different meditation techniques like meditating on the amazing things that God has done in your life and doing breath prayers. I can tell you more about this later.

10. **Journaling**: Write about your thoughts, dreams, and experiences in a unique and creative way, such as through poetry or storytelling.

Exploring these everyday activities in fresh and creative ways can add novelty and excitement to your daily life. Don't get hung up on what you can't do. Do what you can. Explore and enjoy yourself!

I want to remind you that you are not alone. There are people in your life that you haven't allowed to walk with you through some of the hard things that you've been facing but you gotta let them in. I know that you may be thinking, "I don't want to put my problems on them" but I'm here to tell you that You are LOVED!

People WANT to walk with you! You are a Gift and a Gem to someone. Allow someone to be a gift and a gem to you. I really hope you consider this because embracing the love and support of the right people can truly bring comfort, peace, and healing to your heart when dealing with stress and especially when dealing with loss. This is a good segue to begin discussing the thing that none of us want to think about, let alone talk about, and that's loss.

I know that this is an area that may be very raw for you right now. I want you to know that if you don't feel ready to read this portion ***it's okay***. Skip it and come back when you're ready. This is a time when I especially want you to be gentle with yourself. Do what you can when you can and don't do it alone. I'm with you, but it would also be tremendously helpful if you invited someone else that you trust into this space to share your heart and journey with.

Chapter Three:

S. L. A.P.P.'S
....LOSS

Loss tells a beautiful story of love...

LOSS

When we are faced with that empty and lonely feeling that we all get when we have lost someone we love dearly, it feels like it is going to last forever. We know all too well, that broken feeling that we experience, when we have lost someone that means so much to us. It leaves us with what feels like a gaping hole and like we're being forced to start living life from scratch without them.

Most of us know, have known, or will know the feeling of loss at some point in our lives. Although we know with certainty that it will occur, when it does, it's heartrending, distressing, and sometimes earth-shattering sadness is overwhelming. So, we do what we should at times like this. We grieve. Although no one wants to deal with the aching heart and disquieted spirit that comes along with loss. When we embrace and face it, we grow in unimaginable ways.

This difficult season of life brings with it a pivotal experience bearing the potential to bring forth growth in a way that only comes from leaning into the disturbing stirrings within. Realizing that the story you tell yourself is what is going to color the lens in which you see life following this experience. You can decide. You can decide whether you are going to try not to think about the person you loved and lost, or you can decide to remember and share with others the experiences and fun memories that only you know about. You can decide to share the memories of special times of laughter and joy that fill your heart with comfort, love, and happiness.

"Grief is not a sign of weakness nor a lack of faith...It is the price of love."

-Author Unknown

I know that you have prayed and prayed that the pain goes away and when you awake the pain is still there. I know that you wonder why this happened to you and why your faith hasn't healed your broken heart but listen to me. You are grieving and it's okay. You loved immensely and now you are suffering great loss. There is nothing wrong with you. You are not crazy or broken and need to be fixed. You are not doing anything wrong. It just plain ole hurts. I am so sorry that you are so sad but I'm happy that you have had the opportunity to love someone in such a way that your loss is great. This simply means that the person that you lost was important to you and that you had the opportunity to love, to genuinely experience an amazing love relationship with the person who is no longer living. What a Blessing!

'Tis better to have loved and lost than never to have loved at all.

~Alfred Lord Tennyson~

I realize that losing someone that you love hurts immensely but to never experience the honor of loving would be a real tragedy. So, I am saying this to say, don't run away from love because of your pain. Don't deny yourself and others the great opportunity of a real authentic love relationship all for fear of the pain of loss.

During these times we experience our humanity and the brevity of life. We have no power to change the situation, but we can determine how we will allow the situation to change us. We can choose whether we will close ourselves off from living, I mean really living, and loving, or whether we will get back in there and embrace the opportunities we have been given to connect and love again; even with the chance of enduring the pain of possible loss once again.

Enduring the pain of loss can be tricky. During a time of grief, it is important to acknowledge your loss and to grieve but also in that it is equally important not to get stuck in a self-defeating cycle that hinders your healing. You have to feel what you're feeling when you're feeling it, and you also have to find ways to keep living.

You, continuing to live after loss isn't going to cause you to forget about the person that you love, and you don't have to feel guilty about finding ways to continue on. Finding ways to continue living without the person is hard but honors the life that you have and allows you to live and to keep their memory alive as well.

Know this, no one can put a timetable on your grieving cycle. People heal at different times and come to terms with their grief at different paces. Be patient with yourself and know that as long as you are not isolating yourself and are able to share your grieving journey with people who provide healthy and beneficial support, you are processing in a healthy way. A very important thing to know is to never isolate yourself but to do your very best to insulate yourself with life-enhancing relationships.

~ *"Don't Isolate yourself. Insulate yourself with life-enhancing relationships"* ~

I know, when we are sad and hurting right after we experience loss, we don't want to be around other people. We think, please do not hug me! Every time you hug me you make me cry. I am tired of crying! We don't want to keep answering questions about how we're doing or maybe would rather not keep up appearances. We feel like we're trying to make people feel comfortable around the "wounded person." Whatever the case is, I want you to know that it can and will get better, but isolating yourself does not help. You must stick with the plan! Say it out loud ***"Don't Isolate, Insulate."***

When we isolate ourselves from others, we close ourselves off from the joy of being around people who can make us laugh, who we can share memories with, who love us and can empathize with us, and who ultimately want to share the ups and the downs of life with us. Those people are they that *insulate* us! That's friendship. Those are healing relationships! They may not know what to say but their presence means that they care and most importantly that they are here for it all, and that says more than anything that they could ever verbally say. We can all surely use relationships like this in our corner!

Insulate? What do I mean by that? I'm saying allow yourself to be surrounded by people who will protect you during a vulnerable time in your life. Insulation protects and provides a cushion between you and the harsh elements in life that you may be able to handle under normal circumstances but at this time would cause more harm than good.

People who will Listen to you, Encourage you, Laugh with you, Cry with you, Pray with you, be Patient with you, and Correct your negative thinking. ***People who will not let you lay down and stop living.*** People who will keep calling and coming over even when you say you don't want to be bothered. These people provide insulation against the overwhelming desire that comes upon you to quit when things seem unbearable.

Father God, thank you so much for insulating us with healthy, life-giving relationships. We want friends that we can walk with and journey with through the good times and the bad times in life. Help us oh God to recognize those special relationships in our lives and teach us how to cultivate them. We want to have these types of friends and we want to Be these types of friends. We thank you so much for bringing healing into our hearts and for restoring those places that were once broken. Father, we desire to love and to trust again. We desire to LIVE fully LOVING people without fear of suffering the pain of loss. Love is the nectar of life! Thank You for opening our eyes to see how fear tries to steal that from us! Thank you for making us aware of how You strengthen us throughout our journey as we live and love embracing the growth that comes with knowing that You are our healer and that You use us to love one another to a place of wholeness. We love you so much Father, and we give You Praise for healing our hearts and for giving us Beautiful Friends to share our lives with.

Amen

Now, that we've talked about loss and said a prayer to help us to embrace and to be embraced by the loving friendships that God has divinely placed in our lives, let's take a moment to breathe before we start talking about anxiety, the hurricane that subtly creeps into our lives and has the potential to totally wreak havoc.

Let's Breathe...

Close your eyes, inhale deeply and slowly through your nose...and exhale slowly. Inhale deeply and slowly again... and exhale slowly rolling your shoulders back and down. Inhale deeply and slowly again through your nose...and exhale slowly making a sighing sound that sounds like you're getting rid of all of the tension and stress in your body.

That's it... You're doing good. If you need to take a few more deep breaths go for it and when you're ready, we can get started.

Chapter Four:

S.L. A. P.P.'S
....ANXIETY

Anxiety is a storm but within its chaos,
you possess the power to anchor yourself...

ANXIETY

Boy oh boy, anxiety is a slick little devil. I say that because anxiety comes into our lives so subtly that we don't even notice. At first, it masquerades as concern or worry about things anyone would be concerned about. Then we notice that our body begins to respond counter-productively to these "concerns". The slightest bit of concern about anything begins to cause your stomach to feel sick. Your shoulders raise up to your ears, your neck gets tight, and knots begin to form in your back. Sometimes you may get to the place where you feel shaky, sweaty, or even feel your heart racing. Just thinking about this, I need a breather. Okay, let's breathe together again because we have to talk about this.

Alright, breathe deeply.

Inhale slowly...now exhale slowly... Inhale slowly... and exhale slowly...Inhale again... and exhale...one more time, Inhale... and exhale.

Okay, we should be better now. What I just described is a natural response that our bodies have to stress. It's called a stress response. God in His infinite wisdom gave our bodies the ability to be stronger and faster than normal in order to stay alive in dangerous situations. This is what is happening to our bodies during a stress response. Our breathing becomes shallow, our muscles tighten up and our blood stops flowing as normal and is redirected to protecting our vital organs, among other things to prepare us to stay alive in dangerous life-threatening situations. The problem is that anxiety mimics a dangerous situation, and our brains cannot tell the difference between actual or perceived danger. Our bodies react the same way.

I'm going to teach you how to reverse your stress response in a little bit, but I brought up the way that our bodies can react because that experience can be a trip.

You may automatically think that something physical is going on because of the way that you feel and there is, but you can also match your physical symptoms with your thoughts. Your body is responding to your mind. Therefore, I want to present that when we are in a state of anxiety it is fear that is running rampant through our minds. Fear of what could happen. Fear of having no control. Fear of something happening to us that renders us totally helpless. Our minds are screaming DANGER! DANGER!

Imagine this...

Anxiety Speaks

Cold, sweaty, and clammy.

Nervous, shaking and panting.

I gotta get out of here! I need to be able to move around.

I'm on the highway and all I can hear is the sound

of my thoughts screaming inside my head

It hasn't happened, but yet it has, inside as my thoughts race

I feel like my heart can't keep up at this pace

No one knows, no one understands, this
feeling that I have, not even me

Some may say it makes no common sense, but you
are safe! There is no need to be all panicky

The Fear, the dread, the thoughts that I can't fight

Seem so uncontrollable like a bad dream
feels in the middle of the night

I don't know what to do, but Lord I need you!

No one understands what I'm going through

-Priscilla Diane Coffee~

So many people are suffering with anxiety every day. They are so riddled with fear that they are living their lives doing everything they can to make it through the day. Anxiety governs the way that they do life. Let me share a story with you about anxiety in my own family.

One day, my husband was blindsided by anxiety after a trip to the emergency room. We went in because he was having chest pain, but they could find nothing wrong but elevated blood pressure. Well, the emergency room physician decided to mix two medications which he called "a cocktail" that he figured would lower my husband's blood pressure and ease his chest discomfort. As soon as the medication was given through his IV my husband began to feel like he just could not keep still. He felt like he needed to get out of bed and like he just needed to move around. He felt so uncomfortable that he wanted to leave the hospital right away. After the Dr. checked back in with us, he allowed us to leave and that is when it all began.

When we arrived back home, things did not return to normal but were worse. He could not settle down. He walked and walked and walked the floor. He could not sleep, nor could he lay down. Even days after, it was uncomfortable for him for me to touch him, to hold him, or even try to cuddle with and comfort him. Not only that, but we also soon found out that going for a ride in the car had become tremendously difficult for him. If it wasn't a very short distance with him being the driver, he could not handle the car ride. Fear had taken over.

The moment that he lay helpless in that hospital bed with the doctor putting medication in his veins, he felt as if he was being experimented on. He felt like he had lost his power. He felt like he had no control. He felt vulnerable in a way that he had never experienced before. The feeling that he felt in that moment may have been verbally unexplainable, but his body responded with anxiety that took him into a full-blown stress response.

Have you ever felt like you had no control? Have you ever experienced the feeling that your power or your voice had been taken away from you? If you don't know how to verbally respond to such a devastating reality, your body will scream in fear, frustration, and devastation for you. Your mind will react in a way that cannot be ignored. This is a normal reaction to what your body feels is a harmful and abnormal situation. Your mind and body are responding to what it perceives as a threat.

What helped my husband the most was talking about what he was feeling. Facing his fears with great care, with me by his side encouraging, listening to him, and supporting him as he shared with me what was helpful and what was not. We prayed and prayed and prayed some more and we confronted his fears one step at a time. This was truly a time when we had to practice *breathing* through the storm. I know that we often think that when we pray our problems should just go away or maybe our faith isn't strong enough; but let me tell you, that couldn't be further from the truth.

Some things that we face we have to process through, fight through, and breathe through. It's important to know that sometimes in life we are faced with internal threats that may not be actual threats but as I explained before, because our brains think that it is, our bodies respond as if it really is. Allowing ourselves the time, grace, and space to safely work through what's happening in us will help us to gain new perspective and insight that can ultimately prompt our healing journey.

I want to share that as my husband David, and I continued in his healing journey one day he decided that he was going to try to drive a 1.5-hour trip to mom's (his birth mom and my gift from God) house. We both decided that we were going to do what was necessary and accept the small victories while praying and listening to one another. We had decided to take it one step at a time and breathe through whatever came our way.

So, we got on the highway and began our journey. Five miles into the journey, I was on high alert and ready to turn around and head home or pull over at any moment. I was okay with that. I was hoping that we would be able to go further but my mind was prepared to not make it. The thing is, we were headed to Mom's house because we were planning to begin our trip to Virginia for my graduation. This was an 18-hour trip, and we were planning to drive the entire distance in a couple of days. Wow! We were really shooting for the stars. Pretty bold right? The thing is, if we couldn't make it in a car, it would be more difficult on a plane because he couldn't stop and get off when he wanted. So, we went for it!

Twenty minutes into the drive, I was watching him like a hawk. He was taking deep breaths. Inhaling big gulps of air slowly and exhaling slowly. He was trying really hard. I wanted to say, "Sweety it's okay if we need to turn around" but then, I remembered that we discovered that his talking about something that interests him, changes his focus and is a good distraction for him. So, I asked him a question about basketball. He took a deep breath and began talking. It worked! He talked and talked and talked all the way to Mom's house. When we arrived, we could hardly believe it, but we gave thanks to the Lord and enjoyed the evening with Mom. I have to say that I was impressed by the breakthrough but was still concerned with the journey to come.

Morning came and we prepped, prayed, and headed out on our adventure. We were determined to take breaks as needed and to my surprise, it was a beautiful trip. There were a few times when I had to employ the tactic of getting him to talk and engage him with lots of intriguing questions to keep the conversation going but he suffered no anxiety attacks. After the first day of driving, I could see his comfort level rising even to the place where he was okay with being on the passenger side as I drove for a while. It was amazing! We were both blown away by the way that he was able to get through that long trip without any hitches. We felt extremely blessed.

I shared my story with you to share my testimony of God's goodness and faithfulness! When my husband suffered anxiety attacks it was very real and very scary. People experience anxiety in different ways and many people have dealt with it for years and are still searching for a way to be free from the fear of the next attack. I have not personally endured such an attack; however, I have been touched many times with moments of anxiety where I can feel the stress response has been activated.

I am happy to say that no matter how long you have suffered and no matter how many things you have tried to stop your suffering there is good news. There are things that you can do to hack your body to reverse the stress response such as exercising, deep breathing, going outside in nature, and distracting yourself with being mindfully present wherever you are doing whatever you're doing.

Exercise helps to work out the stress hormones that have been released into your body from your brain. It also helps when you take deep breaths. Doing so releases tension from your muscles, and this is good because it helps to calm your body. When you calm your body, you can calm your brain, and vice versa. Being mindful about where you are and what's around you like the 5, 4, 3, 2, 1 exercise that I taught you earlier helps you to notify your brain that you are not in danger, but you are safe wherever you are doing whatever you're currently doing. It works wonders! Also drinking plenty of water helps to flush out those stress hormones. So, think... I gotta flush these extra stress hormones out of my body and do the things that aid you in doing so.

Doing these things helps you to balance your hormones back out so that you can function well again. It's really as simple as that and working on your thoughts. Get into an environment that is supportive. Watch funny videos, listen to music, dance, be around people who take your mind off of what you're worried about, and see your therapist or someone you trust to pray with you and help you process through your emotions.

Most of all, remember that God is our healer. I am in no way insinuating that believers in Jesus don't suffer with anxiety. Nor am I saying that if you are a believer who suffers from anxiety you don't have enough faith. Both of those things could not be further from the truth.

What I am saying is that Jesus is our one and only true healer! He opens up his treasures of wisdom and shares it with people who are in helping professions (doctors, therapists, psychologists, coaches, pastors, etc...) so that they can use the wisdom, education, and skillset that they have to help those who need it when they need it most. They work hard to gain knowledge and understanding of the inner workings of the human body and mind to be God's hands and feet in the earth. God uses them to care for and to bring healing and comfort to those who are hurting.

I'm gonna say it again...Jesus is our healer! Aaand He has placed people on this earth with the education, answers, and support that we need. Open your heart to accept that love and support in human form that the Lord has sent to us in helping professionals.

My husband has not suffered from anxiety in the same way since before our trip and I am eternally grateful. I cannot thank God enough for the amazing breakthrough and healing that he has done and continues to do inside of him.

Now when he experiences feelings of anxiety coming on, he practices some things that he's learned over time that have proven to be really helpful to him. He now has strategies and tools to employ that help him to breathe through difficult times. Here are some things that I learned through that experience:

Anxiety is fear driven. The more one focuses on what they don't want to experience the more they become entrenched in the way of thinking that feeds that very fear. The Bible encourages us in Philippians 4:6-8

Don't worry about anything; instead, pray about everything.

Tell God what you need and thank him for all he has done. Then you will experience God's peace, which exceeds anything we can understand.

His peace will guard your hearts and minds as you live in Christ Jesus.

And now, dear brothers and sisters, one final thing.
Fix your thoughts on what is true, and honorable, and
right, and pure, and lovely, and admirable.

Think about things that are excellent and worthy of praise.

The key here is that the Word tells us that in doing this we will experience the peace of God that exceeds anything that we can understand. The Bible also encourages us in 2 Corinthians 10:4-5

We use God's mighty weapons, not worldly weapons,

to knock down the strongholds of human reasoning
and to destroy false arguments.

We destroy every proud obstacle that keeps people from knowing God.
We capture their rebellious thoughts and teach them to obey Christ.

This shows us how to fight the daily battles that we have in our minds. The thoughts that induce worry, anxiety, and fear (strongholds of human reasoning and false arguments). This is how we use the truth over our rampant worries to fight anxiety. We check those things running through our minds with the truth. When we are attacked by thoughts that try to convince us of our demise, we speak the Word of God which shines light into darkness. We also pray as we strategically apply the wisdom of God to our practical struggles.

I also learned to listen earnestly and not to assume that I knew or understood what my husband was feeling. He was fighting a battle within that I was just seeing and experiencing from the outside. While the enemy was trying his best to fill his heart and his mind with fear, my prayer was that God would help me infuse his heart and his mind with faith and hope. ***The enemy of fear is FAITH.*** When I saw how hard he was trying to make this trip work and how adamant he was about pushing through the anxiety and fear. He infused my heart with hope. I believed that he could do it and my words and actions began to align with that hope.

My husband made phenomenal progress and just as things began to take the shape of some semblance of "normal" in our lives the COVID19 pandemic hit our world. Talk about turning life on its head. COVID19 took our world by storm and shook us all to our very core.

This pandemic brought on stressors that none of us could ever have imagined. Some of which are still affecting many of us today in very different ways. All in all, we've come through and are still coming through one of the most devastating times in our world's history resiliently as a people.

So, my prayer for you is to never lose hope. Fight! Face your fears no matter how scary they may seem. You are living with them every day even when you don't. ***You have nothing to lose and everything to gain!*** Insulate yourself with people who will support and help you through this and prepare for battle! **The end result is YOU WIN!** You may be wondering, *Why is the enemy attacking your peace? Why is he attacking your hope? Why is he attacking your freedom?*

I'll tell you why.

From the very beginning, the devil didn't want you to know who you were and daily he still tries to attack your identity with the lie that "You aren't good enough," with the lie that "God doesn't love you," with the lie that "You are alone" with the lie that "You are a phony and someone's gonna find out" lies, lies, lies.

And you will know the TRUTH and the TRUTH will set you FREE.

John 8:32

You are lavishly loved and chosen by God.

Even before he made the world,

*God loved us and chose us in Christ to be
holy and without fault in his eyes.*

*God decided in advance to adopt us into his own family
by bringing us to himself through Jesus Christ. This is
what he wanted to do, and it gave him great pleasure.*

Ephesians 1:4-5

You are not a mistake. God knows everything about you, and He still chose YOU.

*But God showed his great love for us by sending
Christ to die for us while we were still sinners.*

Romans 5:8

You are and have always been beloved by God. You are here in this world because God chose you. You have a purpose to fulfill every day that you wake up and the last thing that the enemy wants you to do is be bold and courageously live out your purpose!

The scriptures tell us that creation eagerly waits for the manifestation of the sons of God Romans 8:19. Let the light of the

Lord shine through you as you LIVE trusting and believing God even through, especially through your storm.

One of my absolute favorite poems is Footprints in the Sand. I love it so very much because it gives a wonderful depiction of someone who walks with God, enduring pain and suffering, and who feels alone and abandoned by God at times. The poem beautifully describes how God is always with us especially during the most difficult times that we face.

Anxiety may have come into your life but is not here to stay! I am speaking to anxiety right now, and you can say this along with me, out loud for your fears to hear!

Anxiety!

You are an uninvited guest!

You are not welcome in my life!

I am serving you notice!

I am HEALED

I am WHOLE!

I am full of FAITH!

NO THING and NO ONE can stop me from
living a life full of PEACE! JOY! HOPE!

And EXPECTATION!

I am more than a CONQUEROR!

I am a WINNER!

I CAN get through this, and I WILL!

Footprints In The Sand

One night I dreamed a dream.

As I was walking along the beach with my Lord.

Across the dark sky flashed scenes from my life.

For each scene, I noticed two sets of footprints in the sand,

One belonging to me and one to my Lord.

After the last scene of my life flashed before me,

I looked back at the footprints in the sand.

I noticed that at many times along the path of my life,

especially at the very lowest and saddest times,

there was only one set of footprints.

This really troubled me, so I asked the Lord about it.

"Lord, you said once I decided to follow you,

You'd walk with me all the way.

But I noticed that during the saddest and
most troublesome times of my life,

there was only one set of footprints.

I don't understand why, when I needed You
the most, You would leave me."

He whispered, "My precious child, I love
you and will never leave you

Never, ever, during your trials and testing's.

When you saw only one set of footprints,

It was then that I carried you."

~Margaret Fishback Powers

Chapter Five:

S.L.A. P.P.'S
....PAIN & PRESSURE

Pain alerts us, forcing us to pay attention to where we hurt, while pressure shapes us and transforms us in the fire of life's challenges.

PAIN

We all learn early in life that we don't like pain. From our first scrape or bruise to our first heart break in Jr High. We realized that pain sucks. It simply stinks. No one likes it and for good reason. Little did we realize that pain would be a normal part of our life's experiences. It is an unwelcome part for sure but nevertheless, it is a part.

I don't mean to make light of the pain that many of us suffer throughout life but what I do mean to do is to normalize it. I know that sounds crazy but bear with me for a moment. I think I have a revelation about pain. Not wanting to feel pain is normal. It's self-preservation. No one walks around yelling at life saying, "Bring it on! You call that pain! That's all you got! You can do better than that!" Pain hurts. That's the plain old truth. It's because of the way that pain hurts us that we try to avoid it at all costs. But have you considered that maybe, just maybe, pain has its purpose?

There is a pain that comes from injury and brokenness but there is also pain that comes from working on an area of our life, mind, or body that we are not accustomed to working. You know that "it hurts so good kind of pain" It doesn't feel good to me, but it is good for me kind of pain. The intriguing thing is that both kinds of pain have a purpose.

Pain is our alert system physically and emotionally. Pain can trigger us to realize that something is wrong. It alerts us to move quickly to resolve the problem. When we recognize pain, we often respond so quickly that we don't even really think about it before we take action to alleviate the situation. When we take time to discover what the root of the pain is that we are experiencing it can serve us. It can help us to see why pain has come and if the source of the pain is problematic and needs immediate resolution or if it's something that is speaking to us and needs immediate attention.

When we take stock of the things that have occurred in our lives that have brought us tremendous pain, we have to be thankful for our God-given alert system. The pain that was imposed on us while we were in a toxic relationship caused us to not sit in comfort and remain in a relationship that was hurting us. While the pain we endured through experiencing loss allowed us to experience the value of honoring and investing in a loving relationship. That pain helped us to acknowledge that it hurts to lose someone that we love, but we would do it all again just to know and to love them.

Pain that we experience no matter how bad it hurts, serves us. I think that the valuable lesson that pain teaches us is that something is going on that we may not have paid attention to unless we felt the discomfort of pain. Digging into the reason for experiencing pain we can see that pain is helpful. We run from pain like it has come to harm us when the truth of the matter is that the **pain doesn't kill us, it alerts us to live.** Pain is one of our God given Internal Alert Systems that helps us to thrive and to succeed in life. Pain hurts and the next time it comes it will hurt again. Expect it. Embrace it. Find out why it has come and honor your mind and your body by tending to its needs. Pain serves a purpose.

The revelation that I have is that *It is NOT the pain that we fear most*, it is the *reason* the pain has come. The pain has not come to destroy us but the reason for the pain just might if we don't assess why it has come. So maybe we can look at pain and assess it a little differently. Maybe we can look at it as the alert system that it truly is and evaluate why it has come. Maybe we can learn to embrace the pain and not numb it with pain medication so quickly and determine what it is saying to us. Are we in danger physically, emotionally, relationally, or spiritually?

Listen, really listen to the pain in your life right now. Don't drink it away or smoke it away or medicate it away. Listen, really listen, and then deal with it. You have nothing to fear. You've been doing the difficult thing already. This thing has been tearing you up inside and out because you left it unaddressed. Now that you know that the pain is not going to destroy you. I pray that you can find the strength and the courage to deal with the reason why it is here. Pain in most people's eyes has always been something to fear but we just pulled the curtain back and revealed the TRUTH. There is nothing to fear in pain. It hurts. So, let's find out where it came from and why it is here. Pain is simply our God given Internal Alert System saying to us that something is going on so that you will take a look under the hood of your life and assess the situation. Pain is a blessing in disguise. Learn to embrace your IAS and I believe that you will experience peace that brings healing in your mind, emotions and physical body so much sooner than usual. Why? Because now you've learned to pull the curtain back to discover the root of the pain that you feel instead of quieting the thing that has come to help.

There is something else in life that we encounter that acts a little similar to pain and that's pressure. They seem similar, so similar in fact that I remember a very vivid experience of a pressure that I was sure was pain. I went to the doctor for my first womanly check-up, and it hurt... so, my response was like most when we feel pain. I said "ouch! that hurts!" but the Dr said, "you have no nerves here honey that's pressure that you feel. Just try to relax and breathe through it." I thought no way, but I followed her instructions, and the procedure was bearable. I'm not sure how true it is that women have limited nerve endings there, but I could imagine that this would surely make a huge difference during childbirth. God is so Brilliant! He knew exactly what he was doing when He made his children. He made no mistakes!

PRESSURE

Last but definitely not least is Pressure. We experience pressure daily from the silent expectations of family and friends to the written and sometimes implied expectations at our jobs. Life is filled with pressure and to be totally honest most of it is good and helps to push us to be our best selves. With that being said, I have to admit that positive pressure is not the only pressure that we face. Unfortunately, we also deal with toxic pressure. Let's talk about them both.

Although some pressure is toxic and adds no value at all to our lives. It only serves to deplete and sap our energy. It leaves us questioning our self-worth and destroys our confidence in ourselves as well as our trust in others. There are ways to work through toxic pressure. In order to do so, you must identify it for what it is by checking in on yourself.

1. Reflect on patterns: Examine your past experiences and identify recurring patterns where you allowed toxic pressure. Look for common triggers, situations or people in your life that may contribute to this behavior. Understanding the

specific circumstances will allow you to better pinpoint the reasons behind your tendency to allow toxic pressure.

2. Self-Exploration: Explore your beliefs, values, and self-esteem. Consider whether insecurities, fear of rejection, or a desire for approval influence your response to pressure. Understanding your motivations can also give you more insight into why you may be more susceptible to toxic pressure.

I encourage you to explore the patterns that you notice and dig deeper into the way that you see and value yourself in these instances. Don't ignore what you find. Process through your discoveries in prayer, with your therapist or with someone you trust who will listen to you and tell you the truth as well as pray with you and believe God for your healing. You can do this! Release the toxic pressure in your life! It doesn't serve you!

Although toxic pressure is very real and happening in our lives it's a good thing this type of pressure is really a small percentage of the pressure that we all commonly face. I spoke about pressure that pushes us to be our best selves, this type of pressure is positive pressure. It's pressure that shows up in life to help us to perform, to move forward, to do the things that we need to do in life. So, from this point on, we are gonna *look at pressure as a gift and not a rift in the fabric of our lives.*

What is pressure? Well, I like to think of pressure like this: Pressing, constraining, compelling, insisting, provoking, influencing and a continually persisting that either pushes one toward creative prowess and endless possibilities or closes in so tightly on a person that they completely shut down and begin to operate in avoidant behavior. The former is our hope for the pressure that we experience most of the time in life.

I love the possibilities of greatness that I know to derive from pressure, but I do not like the feeling of being pressured. When I'm being pressured, I feel like I'm being rushed and pushed to make a decision about something, and I don't like that because I don't want to choose wrong. I would rather have time to think, contemplate my next move, plan. How about you? Are you okay with pressure or do you dread being pressured? Some people really thrive in high pressure situations, but I wouldn't say that I'm one who welcomes those situations.

I once heard that there are a couple kinds of people in the world; there are those who sit at the table and make decisions & there are those who deal with the consequences of the decisions that others make. Do you think you fit into either of those categories? I don't think that it's that cut and dry, but I do wonder, if you have ever considered that not making a decision **is** in fact a **decision** to not make a decision? If that's true, then making a decision, no matter how uncomfortable, puts the choice in your hands.

I brought that up because making decisions are a necessary part of life and when we don't make them or even put off making them, we live out lives in disarray. You know what I mean? I understand that dealing with pressure can be tough but its necessary for us to learn to work through pressure in order to not be stagnant or stuck in life. This is the pressure that helps us to perform, to pass the classes and graduate, to open the business, or to create amazing things that change the world. Here are a couple of ways to embrace and work through the positive pressure that helps us grow.

1. Set Clear goals:

    a. Define specific and achievable goals. Having a clear roadmap helps provide clear direction and purpose, turning positive pressure into a motivating force.

    b. Break down larger objectives into smaller, manageable tasks allowing you to make progress step by step. This also makes things less daunting, and you are less likely to procrastinate.

2. Develop a growth Mindset:

    a. Embrace challenges and opportunities for growth. View positive pressure as a chance to enhance your skills and capabilities.

    b. Cultivate a mindset that sees challenges as learning experiences rather than threats. This perspective can help you approach pressure with a constructive attitude fostering resilience and adaptability.

What is it about pressure that refines us? I can tell you this. The pressure that refines us causes us to stretch and to grow beyond where we think we can go. This pressure pushes, compels and ignites a fire within that exceeds the ordinary and taps into the extraordinary!

If we embrace this kind of pressure, I believe that we will see ourselves begin to grow and flourish as we are refined through obstacles and challenges that create positive pressure.

Pressure Please

Serve me up a portion of pressure to go with my peas

I don't like it, but I need it because I
won't exceed limits with ease

I want to soar with eagles and be resourceful as seagulls

Pressure + Preparation + Opportunity + Time

Is the base of any great recipe if you desire to excel and shine

Eating is the final part of the creation of a great meal

The most important part is dreaming,
envisioning, and then having the will

To do what it takes to make the ingredients
blend, In the taste testers mouth

Like a symphony of spices converging on
their taste buds testifying of your skill

I need pressure to propel me through opposing
forces and things that would try to hold me back

I'm going forward no matter what comes my
way and in doing so I know I can't slack

On the promises that I made to myself
not just to other people

Pressure can be intimidating but its
advantages have no equal

~Priscilla Diane Coffee~

Courage is grace under pressure.

~Earnest Hemmingway~

When we long for life without difficulties, remind us that oaks grow strong in contrary winds and diamonds are made under pressure.

~Peter Marshall~

Don't be afraid of pressure. Pressure is what transforms a lump of coal into a diamond.

~Nicky Gumbel~

Instincts under pressure crush the carbon of conformity and create diamonds. Each new season of life offers to train us for the next season if we pay attention and adapt.

~T.D. Jakes~

Under pressure, you can win with your mind.

~Tiger Woods~

"Life isn't about waiting for the storm to pass; it's about learning to dance in the rain."

~Vivian Greene

REDEFINE YOUR EXPERIENCE

I know that we often negatively define ourselves by the SLAPP's that we have endured in our lives, but my hope is that since we've gained new perspective, we can begin to explore new and positive ways of seeing ourselves. Especially considering the positive attributes that we've gained as we've persevered and grown through the Stress, Loss, Anxiety, Pain and Pressure that life has thrown our way.

Our SLAPP's have become the "Wind Beneath Our Wings' causing us to soar to new heights. We now realize that "Our problems don't define us, but they Refine us. (Cindy Trimm, 2015, pg.17). We have determined to face any obstacles that come our way and utilize them to our advantage. We seek to mine out the possibilities that those obstacles present. Facing our giants in life only makes us stronger, more resilient, more tenacious, and more fearless!

We are they who dare to take the SLAPP's in life and turn the other cheek saying, "Boy that stung, but now that it's happened, I'm not afraid of it anymore!" We will not allow life's SLAPP's to close us off to opportunities presented to us through opposition, difficulties, complications or barriers. We are they that are willing to go through the conditioning of our minds to STAND and FIGHT! To conquer our fears! To overcome our setbacks! To triumph over our trials! We are they that WIN!

RE-THINK YOUR STORY

In considering all the things that we have discussed in this chapter; we now know who we are. We no longer negatively define ourselves by the SLAPP's we've endured in life. Instead, we seize every opportunity to grow, prosper and excel through them. I think it's time that we rewrite the story that we have been telling ourselves about our life experiences.

How will you rewrite your story?

Every one of us tells ourselves a story about every person, situation and circumstance in our lives. Most of the stories that we have had in our minds concerning the SLAPP's that we've endured, have been negative. We didn't see the value inherent in them, but through this time that we've had together, God has had the opportunity to reveal so much more. The scriptures say,

You intended to harm me, but God intended it all for good...

Genesis 50:20

So, no matter if the SLAPP that you suffered was meant to destroy you. God used it to Bless you! To Strengthen you! To Prepare you for Purpose! To Propel you into your destiny!

I encourage you to consider that you are on the Brink of Breakthrough! You are on the cusp of a Life Altering Revelation that God desires for you to have. Our Father wants you to know that He Loves YOU! And that He called YOU! And that Your Life is NOT a Mistake! He chose YOU! You are here on Purpose! To Fulfill God's Purpose for your Life! You ARE so much Stronger than you know!

Remember...

Take a DEEP Breath...INHALE...and EXHALE

It's okay...You're gonna be okay...

Just Breathe through it!

You can do it!

Okay you Ready?

Let's Keep Going...

In the next chapter, we are gonna talk about embracing and exploring life through the lens of our story!

Enjoy the journey!

Life is happening! Don't stand idly by and let it happen to you. Decide to get in the process and... Let it happen through YOU!

~Priscilla Diane Coffee~

"Success is not final; failure is not fatal: it is the courage to continue that counts."

~Winston S. Churchill

"People do not decide to become extraordinary. They decide to accomplish extraordinary things."

~Edmund Hillary

PRISCILLA DIANE COFFEE

Chapter Six:

WHAT STORY ARE YOU TELLING YOURSELF?

YOUR VIEW OF YOUR LIFE EXPERIENCES ARE CRITICAL TO THE WAY YOU PURSUE YOUR **PURPOSE, CALL and ASSIGNMENT** IN LIFE...

THE POWER OF YOUR STORY

You probably never considered yourself a storyteller but, I am here to inform you that you are. You are one of the biggest storytellers you know. As a matter of fact, it's your very own stories that are the most influential in your life.

There is something so very powerfully inherent in the way that we tell our story. The power does not simply lie in the presentation of our story to others but in the way that we tell our stories to our own selves. You see, it is all in the way that we perceive the circumstances that led to the creation of our story.

So, basically, the way that we tell our story to others is based on how we've told our story to ourselves. You'll find that this is true by examining a past experience in your life that currently shapes the way that you make decisions. This stands to be true whether the experience was positive or negative.

I know that we don't like to think that we can be negative nelly's or pessimistic, but the truth is that once we have experienced something in life that has had a negative effect on us or that's the story that we've told ourselves, we then put in place protective mechanisms to avoid reliving or repeating that same story or outcome again.

Who wouldn't? In the same way, when the outcome of the experience is positive, we also tell ourselves a story surrounding that situation that shapes the way that we proceed in life.

My husband is an Amazing preacher, author and storyteller. As a matter of fact, that's the way that he proposed to me. He told me a story. It was so beautiful. I wish I could tell you the story but trust me, it will take me completely off subject and on a tangent. So, I'll have to tell you about that some other time. But in step with what we are discussing right now, I'll share this life altering story with you. It is the story about what life was like for my husband and I both after testing positive for COVID19.

MY COVID19 STORY

This was a doosy! News reports of COVID19 were everywhere! The world had been shut down for months and finally things seemed to possibly be looking up. Restaurants and stores began to open back up. People were getting more comfortable around one another. People were speaking when they walked by instead of turning their head to breathe in the other direction. It finally seemed as if things were beginning to come around and begin to get back to normal. Little did I realize that the glimmer of hope and desire for everything to get back to normal prompted us to let our guard down, which turned out to be a recipe for disaster.

Our anniversary came and we thought, "let's go out to eat and go for a nice walk in the nature preserve." I love to go for walks. We could be out, see some nature, get a little exercise in, explore the preserve in our new city, all while spending time together doing something other than staying home. It was nothing too extravagant. It seemed pretty harmless and safe to us. I mean we were not travelling or planning to be around a lot of people, so we thought it seemed like a great plan!

So first, we went out to eat. We sat outside on the patio at the restaurant thinking this should be even safer than sitting inside. There were not very many others there, so we thought, "This is a winner." Well, we ate, went to the nature preserve and enjoyed a nice walk.

It was such a great experience that the next couple of days we decided to go for more walks to explore some nice walking paths in our city. We were having such a great time, exploring our city, getting exercise and out of the house at the same time. It was fabulous! I just love, love, love walks. I was in heaven! I started making plans in my mind to eventually explore beaches, zoo's and museums since things seemed to be going so well. And wouldn't you know, everything came to a screeching halt.

Monday rolled around and I could never have fathomed the storm that was coming in with it! I was out getting some work done but at about 10am I didn't feel right. I became progressively worse in a short period of time. So much so, that I said to myself, "I'll just go home early today to rest. Whew I feel weird." I went home and all I could do was get into bed. I woke up with chills. I was hot and then I was cold. I was shaky and weak. My entire body hurt. My skin hurt. My muscles hurt. Everything hurt. I was completely exhausted for days. I could do nothing but eat, sleep, shower and go back to bed. I couldn't even think clearly, my mind was so foggy. I feel like my response time was super slow. I took me a while to gather my thoughts. I was in bed for the next week. I was struggling. I had all the stuff going on but all I could do was take some over the counter medication to try and feel better.

A couple of days into it, my husband David was sick too. He had the same symptoms that I did but he also had chest pain and really bad bouts of shortness of breath. We would literally hold our breath to see if we would begin coughing like the news reports were suggesting we do to see if we had COVID19. We didn't have a cough attack, so we just figured that we didn't have it. We both took NyQuil and DayQuil every day for about a week and a half. Until one day David and I went down for a nap and when we woke up, he sat up on the side of the bed completely drenched with sweat and struggling to catch his breath. We knew we needed to go to the hospital right then to make sure that he was okay.

I was so scared. I knew the stories of people being separated from their loved ones due to the pandemic safety rules, so I made up in my mind that I was gonna be okay, as long as, he was taken care of. When we arrived, the nurses informed me that whenever they called him to go back to be checked on, I would not be able to go back with him. I kind of expected that, but I wasn't as ready as I thought that I would be.

When they called his name, and he began to walk away from me to go back to be seen by the Dr. my heart dropped. I could feel the separation with every step that he took. My eyes welled up with tears and I just sat there. I sat there saying to myself in my head, It's okay, it's okay. It's going to be okay, but it didn't feel okay.

My thoughts were bombarded with **what if's**. All I could think about was, "What if this is the last time, I see him? What if they keep him and he dies in here? I was overcome with sadness. I felt *powerless*. I was scared and alone in Charlotte North Carolina with no family or friends in town with me. Even if they had been here, we couldn't risk anyone getting sick. It's crazy because although I think I am usually pretty well put together when crisis occurs, my rock was taken away from me and I was distraught.

The security guard walked over to me ever so kindly and apologetically asked me to step outside to my car and wait there instead of inside of the waiting room for the safety of myself and others. I complied and began, what felt like the longest walk imaginable, to EXIT the emergency room. At this point, tears flooded my face as I did my best to breathe through these intense feelings of fear and helplessness.

The only thing that helped me a little bit was that we both had our phones and said that we would message one another. I made it to the car and began calling family to inform them of what was happening. They were so loving, kind, supportive and prayerful but in all of their effort to comfort me I remained comfortless. I was experiencing sadness, fear, anxiety, and a sense of loss like I never have experienced before.

It made no sense. I tried all of the things that normally work to give me a sense of calm, but they gave me little to no comfort. My thoughts were bombarded with thoughts of what life would be like without the love of my life. I was sick with sadness. As I'm writing this right now, my heart hurts to think about it. As I relive this moment the air is thick, my shoulders are heavy, and I am deeply saddened. My thoughts, memory and feelings around that evening's experiences were dark, cold, sad and alone.

Five hours later they released David from the emergency room, and we were able to go home and care for one another there. They had diagnosed him with pneumonia, gave him a prescription for an antibiotic and they tested him for COVID19 as well. We waited a couple of days for his test results, and they came back positive. He had COVID19. Seeing this, I thought I had better test as well. Mine came back positive as well. We both had COVID19.

We were home together and that gave us peace. We were determined to do everything that we could to care for one another as best as possible from there. We thought that because of the reports that we had been hearing, 2 weeks should've been the hardest part and that we had been through the thick of it and should start feeling better. NOT TRUE.

It was a scary time for us. Night was the worst. Some days we would both be afraid that it was possible that we would not wake up in the morning. Although we wouldn't even mention it to one another. This virus was the worst! It's hard to reconcile what's happening to you and how you think and feel about what is happening to you. It's interesting how your perception of what you are experiencing can alter your experience altogether. It's amazing how something as simple as your perception can change things for the worse or for the better.

So, since we were home together and were going to have to navigate through whatever came our way; we had to plan for how we were going to work through all that we were feeling in the best way possible. After being an emotional wreck at the hospital, I needed to grab a hold of the reigns of my emotions and take control of what I could take control of. I knew that we were in the storm of a lifetime but since David, my love, got to come home, I felt like we were given an opportunity to live through this craziness on our terms.

So, instead of taking the position of feeling like life is unfair and that the most horrible thing in life is happening to us; we decided to FIGHT by first changing the way that we saw ourselves in our situation. We decided that we were not going to sit by and just let life happen to us, but we were going to engage in the things that we love in life, making the best out of where we were.

We decided to go out on the porch to sit in the sunshine, listen to the bird's chirp, feel the breeze, look at the beautiful sky, trees, and people walking their dogs. We talked to family, listened to music, watched shows together, prayed, worshipped, reminisced and most of all rested. We decided to not let life happen to us but to enjoy the gift of every moment together and allowed life to happen through us! This is precisely what I mean by harnessing the power of the story that you tell yourself.

RE-WRITE YOUR STORY

By changing the way that we saw ourselves in the midst of our fight with COVID19 it changed our perspective from weak, powerless, and at the mercy of this virus to people with purpose who were determined to live life loving one another well and enjoying the beautiful things that we could experience around us.

I also realized that sometimes in life we live with a false sense of security when it comes to living and dying. When that sense of security is ripped away from us and we are faced with the reality of our mortality we freak out because we are forced to acknowledge that we are really powerless over **if** we live or die.

Although the reality of death is something that we all must face at some point we should also be aware of this powerful thing... and that is that **we are not powerless over the way choose to live.**

David and I deciding to be intentional about how we approached each day gave us our power back. Deciding to laugh, video with family, enjoy one another's presence, go out on the balcony and get fresh air, open the blinds to enjoy the sun shining through them was us choosing to live life everyday with intentionality looking for the good things instead of just struggling through the day.

We felt everything, the good and the bad, but we were not so consumed with the bad that we were not able to experience the good. We got through COVID19 "Thank You Jesus!" It was tough and it was scary at times and the symptoms lasted so long we felt like it was lasting forever, but...We Made It! With our HOPE, JOY, LOVE and appreciation for one another and for life intact.

Going through such a life altering experience recalibrated the way that we saw pursuing our purpose in life as things like this often do.

How have life altering experiences changed the way that you see and pursue your purpose in life?

> **Seventy years are given to us! Some even live to eighty. But even the best years are filled with pain and trouble. Soon they disappear, and we fly away.**
>
> **Psalm 90:10**

> **Teach us to realize the brevity of life, so that we may grow in wisdom.**
>
> **Psalm 90:12**

How are you making it through the stress, loss, anxiety, pain, and pressures in your life? S.L.A.P.P.'s are hard and they mark us, but

our scars don't determine our destination in life. They serve as a reminder of where we've been and what we've overcome. When we stop and look at our marks, we will see the faithfulness and love of God, of family, and of friends. We will see our courage in the face of scary things. We will see our determination when it seems as if all was lost. We will see ourselves winning!

We gain so much more than we realize on our life's journey. We don't just win in the ups of life, but we win in the downs. I know that we are always looking to tell that perfect story with no hiccups but that's not life. That's not real life. We have to embrace all of our journey and acknowledge that who we are and will become is directly affected by our journey in its entirety. Not just the pretty parts.

I say this to say, don't be ashamed of your journey. Your journey is what makes you unique. You have the experience that you have because of your journey. You have the wisdom that you have because of your journey. You have the skill set that you have because of your journey. You have the relationships that you have because of your journey. Your life has had its difficult times along with its amazing successes and it all came within your journey.

I think that one of the most powerful things that we can do is to embrace our journey and all that comes with it. As we learn to give ourselves the grace and space to breathe through our most difficult times, we also become aware of and enjoy the good and beautiful things God's placed within every day we are blessed to be a part of.

THE PURSUIT

The way that you view your life's journey is directly related to the way you pursue your purpose, call and assignment in life. As we discussed, if you have determined that life is happening to you and that you have no power or control over what happens in your life; then you walk throughout life living as the victim to your circumstances and situations.

Instead, you should be walking with your heart and mind set on making an impact in the lives of those around you knowing that the pain that you've endured has purpose attached to it.

We all have a purpose to fulfill. Sometimes purpose arises as we redevelop the stories that we've told ourselves about the difficult times that we've endured. It's important that we are aware that it takes intentionality and relentless pursuit to fulfill purpose. I say relentless pursuit because there are so many times when we don't want to share what we've learned through life's challenges. We may not feel qualified or adequate enough to help someone else but, we have to be like Jeremiah when he said,

**"I cannot keep silent… your message burns
in my heart and bones like fire."**

Jeremiah 20:9

Our passion and desire to pursue what we've been called to has to overtake any hesitation connected to fear that we feel in the moment. Someone is waiting for the gift that is inside of you! They are waiting to receive a glimmer of the hope, faith and the grace that has been given to you through the experiences that you've had.

We can't be afraid to share what we have been given. Someone is in need of the hope that comes from your story. It is when you decide to grab a hold of your life; re-write your story and live with intentionality, that you can begin to passionately pursue purpose and impact the lives who need you most.

PURPOSE

Life is so much bigger that we can sometimes fathom. When we are suffering, most times, we feel as if we are all alone but that is not true. Giving purpose to my pain as it pertains to suffering through COVID19 for example...looks like me encouraging and inspiring you to hold your head up no matter what you're facing and choose to live with purpose and intentionality! It looks like me encouraging people to see good things all around them even during the worst of times. It looks like praying for and with people who are suffering and feel alone.

I decided that I would take up this cause because I've faced things that caused me to feel little to no hope at times. I also understand that others are fighting through struggles that I can support them through. So, now I feel called and compelled to inspire people and to infuse hope into their lives. I feel called to encourage people to love themselves well through the challenges they face. I feel called to empower and equip people with the tools they need to live emotionally healthy lives during good and not so good times.

CALL

This call/compelling was birthed out of my own suffering this is what I mean by taking your pain and turning it into purpose. You have some things that you have faced in life that you have told yourself a story about. Rewrite that story and become the Hero in that story as you lean into how you can turn that pain into purpose. When you do you may possibly find your call or compelling to help someone else through the difficulties that you've faced. Imagine what that could look like. Imagine how much healing would flow to you and through you as you look to help someone else.

What do you feel that call/compelling looks like for you?

What are some ways you think you can fulfill that assignment in your life during this season?

ASSIGNMENT

Well for me, I love to pray with and for people. I love to counsel, coach, write, do workshops and retreats. I love supporting and strengthening people through emotionally trying times. I love teaching people how to be emotionally well. I love inspiring, empowering and infusing hope into the lives of the people God allows to cross my path.

Sometimes, I pray live for people on my Facebook page and receive prayer requests. I share emotional wellness strategies and self-care tips on my different social media platforms. I created a course called *The Secret to Building Emotional Strength*. Why? This all came out of me, as a result of, my experiences. This is me exhibiting the power of my story. Now, what about you?

Don't just be a survivor, help someone else. Strengthen someone else. Share the gems that you've mined out of your story to enrich the lives of people around you in whatever way that you can. Take opportunities to breathe life into other people as they face situations that feel insurmountable. Harness the Power of Your Story and impact people within your sphere of influence, however that looks for you.

Chapter Seven:

YOUR HEALING
BEGINS WITHIN

True healing begins within, where self-love and self-discovery transform wounds into inner strength and resilience...

Before You Can See It

The Beauty in Healing

The Wholeness, the Wellbeing, the Peace, The Love

The feelings that come when we know
that the process has finally begun

are Invigorating and Inspiring. It keeps one
Hopeful, Anticipating, Expecting, Aspiring

To be Stronger, Better, Alive, Vibrant and Flourishing.

Seeing yourself thriving when once
under duress is so nourishing

to the heart, the mind, the body and the Spirit.

I didn't see it at first but now I get it!

Healing is seen on the outside, but it is birthed within.

On the inside is where it begins, before it extends

to the outside where people can see

the Beautiful, Precious and Delicate Healing that
God Lovingly and Faithfully began on the

Inside of me

LOVE STARTS HERE

There is something to be said about the way that we love ourselves. We teach people intentionally or unintentionally how we believe we should be treated. I believe that the way that we love and care for ourselves sets the stage for how other people treat us.

Just think about it for a moment. Something as simple as this practical example will prove this thought process as something to consider. Have you ever been in someone's home that was so very well kept that you found yourself being careful not to mess it up in any way? For instance, when you sat down and they offered you something to drink, you dared not sit the cold drink on their coffee table because you didn't want the water dripping from the cool glass to wet the nicely kept table?

There was a study done once about vandalism in a neighborhood where there were abandoned buildings. The kids were breaking windows out in some but not in others. Well, it was identified that where the grass was kept cut and yard clean although those buildings were empty, they were not vandalized. I believe this shows that the way we keep things dictates to others the standard which we hold for them. This in effect causes others, more often than not to show the same respect and regard.

Interesting right? That's definitely food for thought. Now consider that regarding the way you love and care for yourself. Loving and caring for yourself shows others how to respect you and treat you according to your values.

I hope that you don't for one moment think that this is a selfish way to be because it absolutely is not. Loving and caring for yourself is as important as loving and caring for those you love. Seriously. God even vouches for that when He instructs us to love our neighbors as ourselves. But, to truly understand love and how to love ourselves and others well, we have to first understand love. Let's talk about it a little bit.

AGAPE...UNCONDITIONAL LOVE

First of all, I must say that I am a Christian which simply means that I am a follower and lover of Jesus Christ. I know sometimes people have different perceptions of what it means to be a Christian, but to make it plain, I am an imperfect person who loves a Perfect God who loved me first. I'm learning how to love myself and others well every day. God is love and we will never know a more Amazing Love.

As human beings we love with conditions and I understand this because when people hurt us, disappoint us, or misuse us; its protective for us to disconnect, disassociate or completely discard the relationship and them but with God it's different. When I'm not being the best person, He still loves me. He always loved me even before I loved him and that is True for You too. One of my absolute favorite scriptures in the Bible is Romans 5:6-8 because it says,

When we were utterly helpless, Christ came at just the right time and died for us sinners. Now, most people would not be willing to die for an upright person, though someone might perhaps be willing to die for a person who is especially good. But God showed

his great love for us by sending Christ to die for us while we were still sinners.

This is so amazing to me! It's like this... I was guilty of being a sinner and was in court preparing to be sentenced to death and Jesus stood up in the courtroom and said, I know she's guilty, but I will take her place. I'll take her death sentence. Jesus knew that He could take the penalty of death for all of us and rise again with power over death to give all of humanity the opportunity to receive Him and to be reconciled with God. What an Amazing Love!

He saved me from a life of sin and condemnation and most importantly eternal separation from God. All before I knew Him or agreed to follow Him. He also knew that I would flounder and fail on a daily basis, but He Still Loved me. This is a Love that is beyond my imagination. He does such an amazing work in my heart all of the time. Strengthening me and healing me, correcting my wrong thinking, and helping me to be more loving, forgiving and compassionate toward myself and others. I love Him so much! The best decision that I have ever made in my life was to open my heart to receive His love for me.

The Lord loves us relentlessly all of the time. We may know a person who loves really well but they are limited. We have to realize that as people we are imperfect. We mess up but Jesus loves us through it, forgives us and teaches us through our mistakes and ridiculous decisions. He helps us to become more and more like Him when we are willing to follow Him. So, this why I can say as a Christian I am an imperfect person who receives Amazingly Perfect Love from a Perfect God. I'm learning how to love myself and others well from the Best there is.

I shared my love foundation with you so that you can understand the basis of my thought process concerning the matter. This is essential for us to understand because understanding how valuable we are in the eyes of God then sets the stage for how we perceive ourselves. We can begin to clearly see that we don't get our value from our success or lack thereof. We finally understand that we are invaluable.

So, let's just sit with that thought for a moment...

Take a deep breath right here...Inhale slowly...and Exhale relaxing and releasing any tension recognizing the peace of the presence of God.

Doesn't it feel good to know that your value doesn't come from your performance? Thank You Jesus! The great thing is that when we finally understand and receive this grace, we are responsible to extend this same grace to others. The lesson in all of this is that none of us are perfect, but we can learn how to love ourselves and others well daily by being connected to our Loving Savior Jesus Christ.

Therefore, just as I wouldn't be pleased if someone mistreated my child, I believe God feels the same concerning all of us, so the way that we love and care for ourselves is then of great importance to God. Just as the way that we love and care for others is important to God. So, let's talk about how to love others well.

PHILEO...LOVE YOUR NEIGHBOR AS YOURSELF

Many of us have heard the statement, do unto others as you would have them do unto you. Or you may know the scriptures tell you to love your neighbor as yourself. All of our lives we've quoted these things but does this mean? What does this look like in terms of practically living this out? I believe that the way that we treat others is important, while, I also believe that in order to treat others well, you absolutely have to know how to love and care of yourself well.

Matthew 22:37-39 says it like this:

> **37**Jesus replied, "'You must love the Lord your God with all your heart, all your soul, and all your mind.' **38**This is the first and greatest commandment. **39**A second is equally important: *'Love your neighbor as yourself.*

Mark 12:29-31 says it like this:

> **29**Jesus replied, "The most important commandment is this: 'Listen, O Israel! The Lord our God is the one and only Lord. **30**And you must love the Lord your God with all your heart, all your soul, all your mind, and all your strength.' **31**The second is equally important: *'Love your neighbor as yourself.* No other commandment is greater than these."

Luke 10:27 says it like this:

> **27**The man answered, "'You must love the LORD your God with all your heart, all your soul, all your strength, and all your mind.' And, *'Love your neighbor as yourself.*"

Galatians 5:13 says it like this:

> **14**For the whole law can be summed up in this one command: *"**Love your neighbor as yourself**."*

James 2:8 says it like this:

> **8**Yes indeed, it is good when you obey the royal law as found in the Scriptures: *"**Love your neighbor as yourself**."*

I'm showing you this to cement in your mind that God Loves you as much as He Loves other people and He desires that we do the same. Love yourself. It's not more noble to love and care for others while we disregard ourselves. We should be Loving ourselves well. Then and only then can we love others as well as we should.

Give yourself permission to Love yourself better. To take time to care for yourself more. To relax without guilt, drink a cup of tea, take yourself out for a stroll in the park, take a dance class, go to a movie, paint, join a club, or a sports team, read a book, or even take a baking class. Do the thngs that refresh you. I believe when we love ourselves well, we are saying thank you and showing appreciation to God our Creator.

Prayer

Thank You Lord for allowing me to see just how much You Love me. I can see that You desire for me to Love and care for myself as well as I love and care for other people. I understand now that You don't deem it more honorable when I disregard myself in order to care for others. Thank You for teaching me how to do both well. Thank you for allowing me to have this time in Your presence. Thank You for filling my heart. Thank You for releasing me from guilt and condemnation. I receive this revelation and will apply it to my life so that I can honor You by Loving myself well. Thank You Father,

Amen.

SELF-AFFIRMATIONS... CONFESSIONS

A major part of healing and showing love and care for ourselves is the way that we speak to ourselves. Think about this, No one talks to you more than you do. Really! I'm serious! You talk to yourself whether consciously or subconsciously all of the time. Therefore, the things that YOU say to yourself are the most impactful to you! I'm gonna say it again...The things that You say to Yourself are the most impactful to you! Our thoughts are constantly churning and sometimes those very thoughts talk us out of something good without even giving it a chance all because of our self-talk.

So, with that in mind, were gonna talk about self-affirmations and how powerful this practice is. This is something that really needs to be added to your self-care toolbox. You may be thinking that speaking positively doesn't really change anything but I'm here to tell you that it truly does! I'm not just talking about saying positive things for the sake of saying them. I'm talking about confessing, positive, mind shifting, life transforming things to yourself about yourself!

Since we're talking about life transforming, game changing self-affirmations let me put a few rules in place.

1. **Self-Correct Immediately**

Identify and address negative thinking patterns immediately. For example, if you find yourself saying things like; *Nothing good ever happens to me* or *I knew it was too good to be true* or how about this, *Mondays are always my worst days of the week*. STOP. Catch yourself in the act and change what you are confessing.

Say things like,

- I believe something good can happen to me today so I'm keeping my eyes open to see positive things around me.

- I am looking forward to positive changes in my life. I deserve to be happy.

- Monday is going to be a Great Day! I look forward to seeing all that I can accomplish!

2. **Buy into what you're saying!**

Believe that you are worthy of the good things that you say about yourself. Understand that you are training your mind to speak and to look for the positive in every situation instead of the negative. Believe that every moment that you breathe in a new breath is an opportunity for you to embrace a new moment and to change your thoughts to ones that will launch you into a stream of positive thoughts. Positive thoughts lead to hopeful words, that lead to amazing decisions, that guides your behavior ultimately cultivating the Destiny that you so greatly desire for your life.

Here are some Amazing Self-Affirmations. Adjust these to fit your life. These are just a few examples.

- I Love Myself

- I am Beautifully Unique. A Designers original. Invaluable.

- I choose to be hopeful and optimistic.

- I choose to ask for help when I need it and to acknowledge that I'm not alone.

- I refuse to give up when I fail or fall. I'll keep trying until I succeed.

- I trust myself to make the best decision for me

- I am a stronger better me after enduring hardship, difficulty and challenges.

- Today is a New Day filled with New Opportunities.

- I choose friends who are supportive, positively challenging and that treat me well.

- I am compassionate and forgiving to myself and others.

- My thoughts create my reality, so I choose to think about the Best and the Most Beautiful things.

- I am more than good enough, and I get better every day.

- God made me perfectly, flaws and all

- Today is going to be a Great Day!

- Today I will operate at optimal capacity. My Mind is Strong, my Body is Strong, my Spirit is Strong and ready to make a positive Impact on the world around me!

I hope that you begin to talk to yourself with love, patience, encouragement and compassion. Give yourself grace and space to falter and fail. It's a part of living and learning. Forgive yourself and move forward. Have you ever asked God for forgiveness but still let that fault linger over your head? Forgive Yourself and move forward. You have already been forgiven.

FORGIVE (GRACE & SPACE)

I remember reading Colossians 3:13, *"Make allowance for each other's faults, and forgive anyone who offends you. Remember, the Lord forgave you, so you must forgive others."*

I was truly taken aback. I know that God is a loving God and He clearly wants us to forgive one another. I think it was the fact that I realized that we all have faults and would need to acknowledge that we All need to be forgiven at times. This is what truly amazed me. I never considered before that God desires for me to open my heart to forgive others, but he also expects for me to open my heart to forgive myself as well.

I love this so much because as we have been talking about healing in this chapter occurring from the inside out, we have to look at forgiving ourselves and begin to move on with our lives realizing that we have already been forgiven. We must release ourselves from carrying the weight of the burden of punishment for our past faults.

I know that sometimes there have been situations in our lives where we've made terrible decisions that negatively affected or even hurt other people. No one likes to face that. No one likes to admit that, but it's true, and no one is exempt from it. Forgive Yourself.

Let me tell you a secret... You have to forgive yourself first before you ask another person to forgive you. The lifting of that burden from your heart can't solely come from another person forgiving you.

What if they won't forgive you? Will you walk around your entire life unforgiven because of it? No. No. No. Absolutely not. Forgiveness is for you. When we forgive it releases a huge burden and weight from our heart. It frees us from the pain and toxicity that unforgiveness creates. It dismantles hate and self- loathing.

Forgiveness is a gift that we can give to ourselves and to others that releases us from the prison of punishment that we build to enforce penalty upon others and ourselves. Jesus said in John 8:36, *"So if the Son sets you free, you are truly free."* When we can embrace forgiveness this way, we can begin the to heal. You may have never thought about this but you hold the power to initiate healing in others through forgiveness. So, lets talk about embracing forgiving others.

I know that people have hurt you. I know that some things that people have done to you have been so bad that you feel like there's no way that you can forgive them, but just as you need to be released from the prison of unforgiveness. You have the power to release others from the same. When you hold a person captive with unforgiveness you are the jailer so you're in prison as well. Free them and you Free yourself.

Forgiving others is important because it reminds us of our humanity and the fact that we all mess up. Jesus forgave us and expects for us to forgive others.

I know that it's not always easy, but your freedom is worth the effort. Loving ourselves enough to forgive and be healed is worth it. There is a process that we all have to go through. Our feelings don't just vanish, but we can, and we should pursue forgiveness for the sake of being healed from the inside out. I have a few suggestions for pursuing healing.

- Pray and talk to God openly and honestly about how you really feel.

- Cry. Release that pinned up pain. It's okay. Crying doesn't make you weak. Often, we are hurt, and we mask it with anger and hold tightly to unforgiveness in order to protect ourselves.

- Acknowledge how you feel and why you feel the way that you feel. When you can properly identify what you are feeling, you can finally face it, address it and begin your healing journey. Know that NOTHING is too hard for God and that He will give you the Strength you need along with the people you need to get through this.

- Connect with a confidant, someone you trust who will listen to you and pray with you through this difficult time. Express your feelings and your desire to forgive and move forward and partner with them in praying for your healing.

This may be difficult, but You can do it! I'm excited for your journey of forgiveness and healing.

I hope that you have gained insight into how much God loves you. I also hope that you now see the way that you are loving yourself as a response of gratitude to God. I hope that you understand that practicing self-affirmations leads you to positively approach your days filled with hope and positive perspective. Finally, I hope that you have received the desire to forgive and be healed whether you need to forgive yourself or someone else. God wants you FREE.

Chapter Eight:

YOUR RELATIONSHIPS MATTER

Identifying healthy, life-enhancing relationships from ones that are toxic is vital to living and enjoying a vibrant life.

RELATIONSHIPS

I have come to realize just how vital relationships are in our lives. You may not believe it but quality, life-enhancing relationships or the lack thereof impact your life immensely. Ican't stress enough how vitally important it is for us to have good, healthy, life-enhancing relationships. These types of relationships help to sustain our mental and emotional health and wellbeing as well and insulate us through the SLAPP's (Stress, Loss, Anxiety, Pain & Pressure's) that we endure in life.

Throughout life we enter into many different types of relationships. Relationships ebb and flow, they flourish and grow but as you know and may have experienced some are not good, and they end or need to end. That's okay, that's a good thing. The key to having healthy and beneficial relationships is learning how to manage them well.

One of the most important things that we can learn about relationships is how to identify and invest in good ones while also learning to effectively identify and dismiss the toxic ones. In life you get both. You get the good and the bad and that is to be expected. The secret is learning to manage your relationships so that you can maximize the good and alleviate the bad as much as possible.

I know, I know...easier said than done. BUT... It's POSSIBLE. Relationships can be really complex, so knowing how to manage them can really be a game changer.

Sometimes we have really difficult familial relationships and learning to manage those relationships are important in order to maintain good family ties. Sometimes we have friendships where we have hurt one another and don't know how to fix it. So,we give up... thinking that it is unfixable. NOT True. Fixing it is POSSIBLE. Really. Just believing that it is possible can stir up your faith in renewing and restoring what is broken.

Have HOPE in the realization the It's POSSIBLE. Knowing that it's possible opens your heart and mind to dream about the possibilities inherent in rebuilding that relationship. All you need to ask yourself is...

- Is it worth it?
- Will this relationship enhance the quality of my life and I the other person's life?
- Am I willing to put the work in to restore or to rebuild this relationship from the ground up if necessary?

If your answers are emphatically YES then embrace the hope that it is POSSIBLE. Let's talk about it...

RELATIONAL ACCESSIBILITY

Relationships are so important and dare I say consequential to our living a happy, healthy and fruitful life that it's important for us to always assess and then reassess the proximity in which we allow people that we are in relationship with to be to us at any given time.

Okay, I know you're thinking... What in the world are you talking about? Let me explain. We are all human beings, who have to recognize that our environments are important. You can't jump into a swimming pool and expect not to get wet. In the same way, you can't be in close proximity to chronic negativity or toxicity and it not have an effect on you.

People in your life are granted access to you according to what you will allow. You have the key. Not the other way around. I heard my Pastor say one day that "people will get upset with you because you say no to something they want as if you did something wrong to them." Do you see anything wrong with that?

First of all, you have the right to say no. It's yo business... in my Tabitha Brown voice. Really. It's important that we set boundaries and know that the boundaries that we set may not be okay with others but that's just fine. You set them because they were necessary for your wellbeing. You don't have to please others with the choices that you make for your wellbeing.

It's your responsibility to live a healthy and authentic life that you can be pleased with. This is super important because I know waaay tooo many people that live their lives pleasing others and at the end of the day are not happy with who they see in the mirror. You are the one who will be with yourself always. It's hard to live your life being unhappy with the person who is with you every second of your life. YOU

So, assess the relationships in your life by determining where people fit. Ask yourself these questions:

1. What is the Strength of this relationship?
2. What makes this relationship good?
3. How often can I be around this person and things be good?
4. Do I feel respected and valued in this friendship?

5. Is there mutual trust and reliability in our interactions?

6. Are we able to communicate openly and honestly with each other?

7. Do we support each other's personal growth and well-being?

8. Are conflicts and disagreements resolved in a constructive manner?

9. Is this friendship balanced, with both parties giving and receiving equally? (this is not always the case and that's okay as long as the relationship isn't totally one sided)

10. Do I feel comfortable being my authentic self around this friend?

11. Is there a sense of joy and positivity in our interactions?

12. Does the friendship bring out the best in both of us?

13. Are shared values and interests a foundation of this friendship?

Reflecting on these questions can also help you gauge the health and quality of your friendships and identify areas for improvement if needed.

Does this relationship:

1. Make me happy?

2. Help me Grow?

3. Hold me accountable?

4. Hurt me?

5. Make me feel bad?

6. Hold me back in some way?

Asking yourself these questions can help you to assess the relationships that you have and how close you should allow them to be to you and with what regularity. This is not an exhaustive list of questions, but they are some significant things to consider.

Because life has twists and turns that we all endure there are times in life where even the people we love may not be the best people to be around for a time. We have to understand that when someone is going through a rough patch, we may need to control the access that they have to our lives for a season so that we remain emotionally healthy. That may not mean that this will be forever, but it does mean that you have the choice.

I'm mentioning this because sometimes people we love dearly become toxic to our emotional health and we have to set some boundaries that control the access that they have to us. This is okay. This is good for you, and it is good for them. This is a way to protect your peace and a way to salvage a relationship that may otherwise be damaged if you don't make the necessary adjustments.

That is why we have to assess and when necessary, reassess our relationships to be sure that they are healthy and headed in the right direction. I define healthy as respectful, helpful, loving, generous, kind, honest, and compassionate among other things that I value. *How do you define a healthy relationship?*

While I understand that each of my relationships are unique, I do have expectations of the relationships that I allow to be in close proximity to me that keeps me well and those relationships well.

Check this out. I want you to understand that your needs may change from time to time based upon what you're going through in life. Meaning, if someone close to me is struggling and I'm okay and feel like I have the capacity to walk alongside them through their difficult time, I will. Why? because I feel emotionally capable of being there with and for them. I don't take their burden and place it on my shoulders and carry the weight of it as if it were mine, but I love them, pray with them and support them in any way that I can.

On the other hand, when I feel emotionally fragile, I have to know this and not take on this type of responsibility because I put myself as well as put the relationship in a compromising position. Have you ever resented a person because you felt like they should have known that they were asking too much of you or putting too much on you? This is what happens when we are not aware of where we are emotionally and don't assess the relationships that are in close proximity to us when we need to. It's not their fault but it is our responsibility to be aware of our emotional capacity so that we can manage our relationships well.

Just something to chew on.

I know your brain is swirling right now...Come on and take a breath with me...

> **Inhale slowly...and Exhale.... Inhale slowly again rolling your shoulders back and down.... And Exhale...one more time Inhale slowly...and Exhale releasing all of the tension that you're feeling.**

Okay, you got this...Take some time and assess your relationships and when you need to, Re-Assess them. It's a continual thing... It's a part of Relationship Maintenance. This is a powerful way to manage and keep your Relationships Healthy.

Listen. I want you to know that investing in healthy relationships begins with investing in yourself. You have to first know who you are. Second, know what you need out of the relationship, and third, know what you are willing to contribute in order to have a healthy and mutually beneficial relationship.

YOU LEAD

Alright, first things first. I mentioned that first you need to know who you are. I said that because so often in life we get caught up in other people's perception of us. We begin to buy into it and move in that relationship under false pretenses. Basically, FAKE. Life is too precious for us to walk around living inauthentically.

The best gift that you can give to yourself and to others is the REAL YOU. Flaws and all. The terrible thing is that this misconception generally comes from within us. It's not the other person's fault. It's ours. It's what we call people pleasing. When a person is unsure of themselves or struggles with low self-esteem or low self-worth, they develop keen people pleasing senses and before you know it, they build most of their relationships according to what they feel like others want to see or hear from them.

Living life this way is mentally and emotionally draining. It seems as if no one sees you or really cares about you or your needs but the truth is that no one really knows. They don't know who you really are or how you really feel.

"It takes courage to grow up and become who you really are."

~E.E. Cummings

This is exactly why being unapologetically YOU in all of your relationships is important. Yes, you are flawed. Join the club! We all are! Be bold. Be courageous. Be You in all of your splendor! Sometimes that's the creative thinker, mover and shaker, brilliant you. Sometimes that's fun, jokey, laugh till you cry, silly you. Sometimes that's the contemplative or the sad you. Sometimes that's the excited, loud, over the top, joyful you. Sometimes that's the angry you. Whatever it looks like, just as long as it is YOU.

You'll feel good about it. Why? Because it's authentic. You won't feel like you have to pretend in order to keep the relationship. Anyone in a relationship with you needs to be in relationship with YOU not a bad imitation of you. You are enough just the way that you are. Don't let people miss out on getting to know you. There is only One You and that's all this world will ever get. Let us embrace the Real You. We can handle it!

Now the next thing is to know what you need out of your relationships. While this may sound tricky it isn't. It's actually quite simple. These are the intangibles that you know that you need and want but may not verbalize.

I'm talking about things that you value in a relationship like honesty, and kindness. Maybe you value loyalty, patience, faithfulness, or optimism. Sometimes we want something or need something, and we assume that the other person should know what we need. That's not okay, nor is it fair to you or to them. When we don't verbalize what we expect, what we want or what we need, people will disappoint us over and over again. It doesn't have to be that way. Communication is key. We have to communicate our needs to people we are in a relationship with otherwise we force them into a position where they are a continual disappointment to us, and we unintentionally sabotage that relationship.

Say for instance, you value optimism, and you have a friend who always complains and looks at life pessimistically. You will dread having a conversation with this friend because you may feel like they bring you down with negativity every time you talk to them. This friend would not be aware of this if you don't share it with them because they are not doing this to hurt, frustrate or hinder you. Frankly, they are not even aware that it does. This may feel like a difficult thing to work through but approaching this situation from a position of love for your relationship and with a mindset of how to make it better for the both of you will give you the creativity and grace that you need to save this relationship.

A Lack of Communication creates misunderstandings which ultimately puts the friendship in danger.

~David Coffee

What do you need from your relationships? You will need different things from different relationships, but you must identify what that is you need in each relationship. It's gonna help so much! A great example of how to do this is first exploring the strengths of your relationships.

This is what I mean. If you have a friend that you hang out with, laugh a lot with, and maybe even go on outings with like hiking etc... these things may very well be the strengths of your relationship with that person. Enjoy those things with that person. Don't expect them to be a listening ear when you're having problems in your romantic relationship and give you good advice. That may not be the strength of that relationship. You're gonna be upset because you can't get that from this person. What you can get is a reprieve from stress by having a great time and that's wonderful. Embrace that and enjoy this relationship for what it is.

Finally, you have to know what you are willing to contribute to the relationship in order to have a healthy and life enhancing relationship. We're gonna talk about life enhancing relationships in a second but right now, I want to focus on your contribution in your relationships. We identified that we need certain things from others in our relationships but what are we prepared to contribute to our relationships to be sure that they are healthy?

Be the kind of friend that you want to have in your life.

We need people and people need us. Life was not intended for us to live alone. When we share life with others that requires give and take. Mutual contribution. While we consider what it is we need in relationships with others, we must also carefully consider how we will contribute to the relationship to build up and strengthen those relational bonds.

Life is better when we go at it together. I may never see the things that you have seen, go the places you have gone nor have the experiences that you have had, but because we are in relationship, I gain insight and experiences that I would never have had, had we not been friends and vice versa.

When considering being an active contributor in your relationships think about your relationships and what those people need right now through your friendship. What are you prepared to give? It could be patience, encouragement, a listening ear, a positive challenge or something else. Can you identify what your relationships need from you most right now? Think about it. You can have a conversation with your friends or family asking them how you can be a better or more supportive friend, a better spouse, a better sibling, or a better parent to them. You can ask if there was one thing you could do to be more supportive what would that be? You are not obligated to do exactly what they say but you can talk about it. It will open communication because you care enough to ask. Happy asking!

LIFE ENHANCING RELATIONSHIPS...

"Your greatest gifts walk into your life on two legs"

~Dr. Dharius Daniels

We often think that the most wonderful things that can happen to us or for us come in some form of us being celebrated or elevated, but I have news for you. One of the most beautiful, humbling, and powerful gifts that we could ever have are relationships. Relationships have the capacity to make us better people. They have the ability to help us to walk in purpose. They strengthen and mold us in ways that could only happen through living life alongside other imperfect human beings.

When I say imperfect human beings, I mean all of us. I know that we have a tendency to want to be seen as without flaw or at least being close to perfect most of the time but let me tell you now, you're not. We might as well just get this out of the way. You are not perfect, and neither am I. No one is. I hope that's a relief!

The beauty of it all is that we have the opportunity to live our lives in authentic relationships with other people as we all grow and mature as human beings. It takes us being okay with loving and sharing our imperfect lives. This means the good and the not so good, because believe it or not the difficult things that we face in life can be life lessons that give support, hope and healing to others if we dare to share. Living authentically and at times transparently has the potential to enrich our lives as well as the lives of the people with whom we are in relationship with. You may be thinking, "okay, I don't know about all of that" but hold on a second…let me tell you what I mean.

As we are living our lives, we are impacted in so many ways by the people that we do life with. Likewise, we touch lives and leave an imprint in the lives of the people that we are in relationship with as well. Sometimes those imprints are good and sometimes they are not, but my hope is to leave a mark that is good and memorable in the lives of the people that I am blessed to encounter. Not so that people remember me, but so that they remember the good and impactful things about our encounters. My hope is that God uses me to allow people to feel seen, heard, cared for and loved in some way. *How about you? How do you want people to feel or what do you want them to remember about their encounters with you?* There are many life-enhancing relationships, but I want to specifically take a moment to talk a little bit about Mentors, Mentees and Confidants.

Mentors show up in our lives as Pastors, Teachers, Coaches, Supervisors, or people who have something that we desire to have, like amazing marriages or great business models just to name a few. We often identify these people as people that we honor and respect and can listen to and learn from. This is great because we are always developing into better versions of ourselves and it's important to always have a picture of our next goal for growth in front of us. And by this, I mean a picture of a person who is living and doing what we desire to add to our lives. Remember, they don't have to be perfect. That's not what we are looking for or expecting from human beings.

Mentors shave time off our endeavors so that we don't have to re-invent the wheel so to speak. We can learn from their years of experience, bumps, bruises, failures, and successes. *Have you opened yourself up to advancing in the area of personal development by embracing the life enhancing relationship of a mentor?* I hope so. If not jump on board because you are definitely missing out on a major advantage if you have yet to do this.

If having a mentor is a concept that you are struggling with you are not alone. Unfortunately, a lot of people do because they look at themselves as having an inadequacy because of their need for someone's support. That is absolutely not true. Sometimes we inaccurately think that because we are adults that we should already know most things or be able to figure things out on our own and that is not true.

We don't know what we don't know and that's okay. We're never going to know everything, and we're not supposed to. We can't continue to treat ourselves as though we are coming up short of who we are supposed to be if we don't know or are not good at something. We all need support in different areas of our lives. That's why God made us to be interdependent. We need each other. We are better together. We don't have to go at life alone. I'm saying this hoping to encourage you to lean on someone. Open yourself up to being mentored and enrich your life. Speaking of enriching your life, mentoring someone else (a mentee) is an amazing blessing for you as well as for them.

Can you see yourself as someone's mentor? You have years of experience, bumps, bruises, failures, and successes in different areas of your life that someone can benefit from if you are willing to open up and share those parts of your life with someone who needs it.

Mentees enrich our lives because we share the gems that we've learned through our life's journey with them in a way that saves them time, money, heartache and sleepless nights. Mentoring also feels purposeful to us and that feels good.

Imagine taking the things that you've gone through and sharing pitfalls with others so that they don't fall into the same traps that you did. It's so rewarding. It kinda feels like you're making the enemy pay for all of the trouble that you endured by revealing traps and snares to other people who would otherwise suffer.

I love it! It's the cheat code! My philosophy is to give what's been given to me. Sharing the information that I have and experiences that I've had that will help others is important to me because I want people to WIN! I want people to be healed and to live empowered lives. It fills my heart so much to know that I have the ability to enrich someone else's life by being open to sharing mine. This brings me to another way of enriching someone's life that may not seem like a big deal, but it is a very big deal and that is being a Confidant.

When someone can trust you to hold a confidence that means that they trust you to listen to them during some of the most difficult times of their life. I know that when you hear it like this it sounds HUGE. It is. All of us have a need to feel heard and cared for and this is what you provide to people when they can confide in you. Your presence and your listening ear give a sense of comfort and care to a friend who needs to share sensitive information about their lives with you.

The person sharing usually doesn't need you to fix it. Although sometimes we feel like we need to find a way to take the pain or frustration away from the person that we care so much about. That's most likely not why they came to you. They came to you because they trust you and because you've shown that you care. This is a good thing.

Being a confidant is important and identifying who in your life you can trust and confide in when you need to talk is important as well. These precious relationships can help us through some of the most devastating times in life. These relationships are invaluable and enrich our lives in ways that we can hardly describe. If you have a relationship like this, treasure it. And if you can be this for someone else count it as a blessing and hold it close to your heart. There is something very important to note about these relationships though.

You have to be very careful to have boundaries that protect your peace and your emotional health.

Protecting your peace may look like not allowing a person to share their load with you if you are already in a vulnerable place emotionally. You have to be self-aware enough to know that something added to your emotional plate right now will be too much and that's okay. We talked a little about this earlier. That does not make you a bad friend, but it makes you a kind, compassionate person to your friend as well as to yourself. It's not ONLY important to care for your outward relationships but it is also paramount that you take care of your most consequential relationship and that's your inner relationship... your relationship with yourself.

Maybe taking care of yourself emotionally has not been a priority for you in the past but hopefully now this is something that you will change with intentionality. I say with intentionality because if you don't put a plan in place to ensure that you set up boundaries to keep your peace and to invest in taking better care of yourself, it won't happen. I encourage you to make taking time to take better care of yourself non-negotiable. You'll show up in life as a better you, for yourself first and then for the people and for the things that you care about the most.

BE THE FRIEND YOU DESIRE
TO HAVE IN YOUR LIFE

To gain a friend we must first show ourselves to be friendly.

Proverbs 18:24

As you think about the things that we discussed regarding setting boundaries. I want you to remember that too goes both ways. It's important to honor the boundaries that people in our lives set and not violate them. We have to show honor and respect to others in the same way that we would like to be honored and respected.

This is not the path of thinking most often travelled but it's time to be different. We want healthy, life enhancing relationships and that means that we have to mature. We gotta grow up and stop thinking me, me, me. We have to think of life and relationships in a fuller picture. We have to walk into our relationships with our eyes open and with wonderment asking God,

- How can I enhance this person's life?

- How can I love them well?

- How can I encourage, inspire and support them well?

And live into that. You got this! You can do this! I know you can!

This is what I want you to remember...

Life enhancing relationships are possible. No matter how difficult things have been up till now. I hope you've gained insight into how you can more healthily manage the relationships most important to you.

Another thing is to be YOURSELF. No relationship is worth you needing to pretend to be someone that you're not. Without you being you, the world is missing out on you and all that you are. We need you to be you. You need you, to be YOU.

Finally, find ways to invest in relationships that enhance your life and find ways to enhance the lives of others. Let it be said that you left an indelible mark in the lives of the people you've encountered for the Glory of God!

Chapter Nine:

ARE YOU LISTENING TO YOURSELF?

Amidst all the noise of the world, listen to the symphony within. Your inner voice, your compass of truth guiding you towards authenticity.

LIVING IN ALIGNMENT

It's one thing to feel unheard by others but what if I told you that you often don't even listen to yourself. We all have a need to be heard and cared for. Wanting to be heard by the people in our lives is a natural thing but what often seems to be missing is the art of us first listening to ourselves. We can't expect that other people will listen to us and understand and tend to our needs until we first understand and tend to our own needs.

For example, have you ever said that you were going to stop spending excessive amounts of time on social media and spend more time doing things that are more productive? Or decided that you were no longer going to work long hours because you wanted to spend more time with family? If those things don't grab you this one might. Have you said that you were going to take better care of your health but still overeat and put off working out? I know most of us fit that category at times.

The reason for me bringing these things up is because I want to show you how sometimes we wrestle with what psychology defines as cognitive dissonance. We desire one thing and behave like another. We behave in a way that is not in alignment with what we value. We aren't listening to ourselves. My gramma would have said it like this..." You must didn't hear me... cause if you did, you wouldn't still be sitting there. You woulda did what I said!" Ha ha haaaaa... I got a real good laugh right there cause I said it to my kids too! Ah haa haa haaa!

Okay, so back to what I was saying. When what we want is not in alignment with what we're doing we are experiencing cognitive dissonance or disagreement within ourselves. You see where I'm going with that?

In order for you to begin to move in alignment with what you desire. You're gonna need to decide that you are going to start listening to yourself. You do this by taking inventory of what you value and aligning your behavior with that. When you take inventory of what you value you want to ask yourself...

1. Why is this important to me?

2. What will my life look like if I align my life with this value?

3. What will my life look like if I don't?

4. How will aligning my life with this value make me feel?

Asking yourself these questions will help you to get clear on the things that you value and will also help you to define the feeling that you expect to experience when you align your life with these values. When your thoughts, your feelings and your behavior line up you are unstoppable. Try it and see how well this works for you!

Another way that I like to help people begin to listen to themselves is by doing a self-check. I learned this one day when I was listening to one of my favorite podcasts, The Kwik Brain podcast. Jim Kwik had Mel Robbins on as a guest and she was talking about a way that she learned to check in on herself and I loved it! She talked about how she decided that in the morning when she looked in the mirror, instead of berating herself about how she had dark rings around her eyes or blemishes on her face she would instead look into her eyes and ask herself "How are you doing today?" This is how I remember it anyway. So, I tried it and I love it sooo much!

Have you ever heard that your eyes are windows to your soul? When you look at yourself in the mirror, look right into your eyes and ask yourself ...

- How are you doing?
- How do you feel today?
- What can I do for you today to make your day better?

Honestly answer yourself. Agree to do what you tell yourself you need and then keep your promise to yourself. We don't easily break promises to others but we too easily break promises to ourselves. Decide to end that today.

If you need a nap say so and then plan when you can squeeze it in your day. Look forward to it and then do it! Doesn't that just sound good? If you need to go for a walk and enjoy the breeze, plan how you can get it in and do it! If you need to call your best friend and reminisce or laugh until you cry, plan when and then do it! Do you need to listen to your favorite song and dance like nobody's watching or sing like nobody's listening? Do it!

The beauty of this is that by doing this, you begin practicing self-awareness and this sets the stage for good self-care. We're gonna talk more about self-care in the next chapter.

YOUR MIND, WILL & EMOTIONS

Do not copy the behavior and customs of this worldbut let God transform you into a new person by changing the way that you think. Then you will learn to know God's will for you, which is good and pleasing and perfect.

Romans 12:2

I loved when I found out that the Bible says that we should let God transforms us by changing the way that we think. This is so wonderful because this says that we are one decision away from allowing our thoughts to change, which will in turn can transform our lives at any given moment. Isn't that Powerful?

This also reminds us that as we do well in life, we are Shining Bright for God. People look at us and see God doing great things in and through our lives.

It pleases God for us to take good care of ourselves. We can both love ourselves and others well. We don't have to choose one or the other. Think about that for a moment. How often have you sacrificed your wellbeing for the sake of "being there for someone else?" I said it before, and I will say it again. We are charged by God to Love our neighbor **as** ourselves not more than ourselves. Let that sit for a minute.

Remember this, listening to yourself is a way to begin to practice self-awareness. This is essential to your growth and development as a person but is also a very important step in your journey towards healing. No one knows what you need like you do and no one is responsible for knowing what you need before you do. If you know what you need you can either give yourself what you need or articulate it to someone who can be there to support, you. We don't become experts at this overnight. It's an ongoing learning process and practice that looks different in different seasons of life. Love yourself well by listening to yourself to determine what you need and when you need it.

Chapter Ten:

SELF-CARE ISN'T SELFISH

Self-care is not selfish, it's an act of loving and caring for yourself in a way that refreshes your mind, body and spirit.

YOU ARE WORTH IT

Oh, my goodness...let me tell you something. I can't stress this enough. You are sooo worth every ounce of time you spend taking care of yourself.

Your family is better because you're in it. Your workplace is better because you're there. Your friends are better because they are in a relationship with you. Your neighborhood, city. state, country and the world are better because God put you in it. We love you and are sooo glad that you are here. No one can be you or do the things you do the way that you do it and that's why we need you to take good care of yourself.

I hope what you've read so far has convinced you that you are loved, valued and needed. In order for you to show up in life for the people you love and for the things that you feel called and compelled to do you need to show up in life as your best self. You have to first show up for you and that's what self-care is all about. Taking good care of yourself.

We're going to take some time to talk about how this looks in four consequential areas of your life. These pillars I like to call REPS because like in strength training the more you practice being well in these areas the more you will begin to see a stronger, more resilient you. We talked about relationships earlier but now I want to highlight a few things to aim for as it pertains to Relational wellness goals.

RELATIONAL WELLNESS

Relational wellness is crucial for maintaining healthy, fulfilling relationships. Relationships are the very way that God has given us all to assist one another in maturing and fulfilling our purpose in life. I believe that relationships are one of the most challenging yet satisfying things that we have in this life. People see us at our worst and at our best and we them. The challenge is to live loving and forgiving lives understanding that all human beings are flawed, and we all need love, understanding and forgiveness.

> *Always be humble and gentle. Be patient with each other, making allowance for each other's faults because of your love.*
>
> *Ephesians 4:2*

A few ways that we can be relationally well is to:

ఱ Practice Effective Communication

- ▸ Strive for open, honest and empathetic communication with the people that you care about
  - • This means listening well (Practice not interrupting and confirm what the person is trying to express. Don't make assumptions)
  - • This also means expressing your thoughts and feelings clearly. (Don't assume that they should already know how you feel).

ఱ Setting healthy Boundaries that protect your relationships

- ▸ Clearly define your personal boundaries

- Express what you like and don't like and also what you want and don't want

  ▸ This also means respecting the boundaries of others creating healthy balance in your relationships

🔖 Letting your voice be heard by practicing Conflict Resolution

  ▸ Learn and practice healthy ways to resolve conflict, focus on finding mutually beneficial solutions when possible while most importantly remaining respectful to one another.

    - Remember allowing your voice to be heard is important. So, express yourself because the way that you feel is going to come out one way or another. Make sure it's in a way that you can be pleased with when all is said and done.

🔖 Spending Quality time with the people you love.

  ▸ Make an effort to spend quality time with the people who matter most to you. Nuture the bonds and connections in your relationships.

🔖 Become a source of Support and Encouragement

  ▸ Be a source of support and encouragement for your loved ones and also for the people that you are in relationship with. Let God use you to impact someone's life. You never know what people are going through. Allow God to express His love and care for someone in their time of need through you. God uses people to Bless people.

This list is not exhaustive but it's a good place to start. I hope it has your wheels turning. Now, let's talk about emotional wellness.

EMOTIONAL WELLNESS

Practicing ways to be emotionally well is also essential for your overall health and wellbeing. Every day we wake up we clean ourselves up, we eat, and we sleep. In between those things we are living a life that can be super tough. We have to build emotional resilience so that we can stay hopeful and joyful in a world that is full of chaos. In a world that is so fast paced and is constantly pulling us in every direction, we have to design our lives in a way that fights for our emotional wellbeing.

Here are a few Emotional Wellness goals to consider:

❧ Practicing Self-Compassion

▸ Be kind and understanding to yourself, just as you would a friend.

▸ Show yourself some extra love and grace during difficult times.

❧ Practicing Positive Confessions

▸ What you say to yourself matters so practice saying good things to yourself. This may take a lot of practice especially if you are used to being hard on yourself, but the good news is the more you practice the better you become. Start loving yourself well, starting with the things that you say to yourself!

Managing Stress Well

▶ Start implementing stress management techniques like mindfulness, meditation and deep breathing into your life to help you to cope with daily stressors.

Embracing Resilience

▶ This is really developing the ability to bounce back from setbacks and challenges, understanding that you adapt and grow from difficult experiences.

▶ Recognize that you will face difficult things and that's just a part of life. Learning how to recover well is the key.

Becoming Optimistic

▶ Expect and look for good things to happen in your life and celebrate them as they occur. You don't have to wait for something monumental to happen to celebrate, celebrate the small things.

▶ Expect the best from people and find ways to appreciate them for the goodness they bring into your life.

Cultivating Gratitude

▶ Practice remembering the victories you've experienced in your life, the year, the month, the week, and the day. Sit in that feeling of thankfulness to God. This reminds you of Gods faithfulness and fills your heart with faith, hope and courage to hold on and continue trusting God on no matter what things currently look like knowing that if He did it before he will do it again!

   Seek professional support when needed.

> ▸ Understand that seeking support from a therapist or emotional wellness coach or counselor is a sign of strength, NOT weakness. Don't hesitate to reach out when facing emotional challenges that require professional support. God gave them the skillset, compassion and call to care for and to support you when you need it most. You don't have to wait for the Lord's voice to crack the sky. Accept His hands and heart in the form of people and let them support you in your time of need.

Emotional wellness is an ongoing journey. I hope you implement some of the things you found from this list that will improve your emotional wellbeing.

PHYSICAL WELLNESS

Physical wellness is also a key component to your overall wellbeing. Take a look at some of these goals that will help you maintain a healthy and active lifestyle.

1. Regular Exercise

> ▸ Engaging in regular physical activity strengthens your body, protects against chronic disease, aids in memory and brain function, improves your mood, improves your quality of sleep, reduces feelings of stress, anxiety, depression and so much more.
>
> > • Implement cardiovascular exercises like walking, jogging, swimming, biking, dancing, boxing, playing basketball, tennis etc...

- Implement Strength training exercises like push-ups, squats, lunges, weightlifting, planks etc...
- Implement flexibility workouts like yoga, stretching, tai chi, etc...

Good Nutrition

▸ Embrace a diet rich in fruit and vegetables and that limits sugary, fatty foods. Basically, try your best to give your body the nutrition that it needs to heal well and to function at its highest capacity.

Adequate Hydration

▸ Drink enough water daily to stay properly hydrated to support your bodily functions. You'll feel so much better when you do.

Sufficient Sleep

▸ Aim for 7-9 hours per night of quality sleep so that your body and mind can rest and recover well and function at its highest capacity. Our bodies heal when we sleep so rest up, don't cheat yourself on your zzzzz's

▸ Creating a sleep routine may be helpful in setting an atmosphere to settle down at night and to get the most restful sleep possible.

Regular medical check-ups

▸ This may not be popular but is important. Regular check-ups and screenings help us to catch and address health issues early. Get your check-ups!

Physical wellness is a lifelong journey. Implementing these goals can help you maintain good health and wellbeing throughout your life.

SPIRITUAL WELLNESS

Love God, love yourself and love others.

Love the Lord your God with all your heart and with all your soul and with all your mind and with all your strength. The second is this: 'Love your neighbor as yourself. "There is no commandment greater than these."

Mark 12:30-31

Spiritual wellness speaks to your relationship with God which touches the inner most part of who you are. Your spirituality determines your value system and the way that you see and love yourself and others. So, right here is where we're going to talk a little bit about a few Spiritual wellness goals.

1. Getting into the presence of God

This may look different for different people and even for you in different seasons of your life and that's okay. That's living and loving Jesus. Don't get stuck on the I used to do it like this...and the I want to get back to the way I used to... The question is:

- How can you embrace your time with God now?
- How can you live and breathe and love him with all of your heart and all of your life in this season of life?
- What best works for you now?

Live into that and love God with all of your heart right there. There is no need to condemn yourself. Be kind and compassionate to yourself.

So now there is no condemnation for those who belong to Christ Jesus. And because you belong to him, the power of the life-giving Spirit has freed you from the power of sin that leads to death. Romans 8:1-2

> ***Come on and just Breathe right there... Inhale slowly and then Exhale. Receive it. Receive the Peace of God right there.***

God Loves you and knows that you love Him. Creating space to spend time with Him is important because it removes the junk that gets on us every day that weighs us down. Spending time with God creates an opportunity for us to be showered and refreshed in His presence.

Refresh me Oh Lord

Refresh me oh Lord, I'm tired and know that I need you.

Refresh me father, I've tried everything but nothings working, I don't know what to do.

Refresh me oh Lord, I feel like I fish out of water the air is thick and it's hard to breathe.

Refresh me oh Lord, It's been hard to get into your presence but I know that it's YOU that I need

Refresh me Father, its you that my heart longs for

Refresh me oh Lord, I can see now that stopping whatever I'm doing to be with You is something that I can no longer ignore.

Refresh me oh Lord, I know that in your presence the sun shines brighter and my heart is lighter.

You are truly my soul igniter.

Refresh me oh Lord, I know what I need to do and I'm struggling to get to it

I'm asking You because it's You that gives me the strength to Will and to Do so that I can get through it

Refresh me oh Lord, I know that it's your breath that I need and long for

Father it's the Healing, Joy and Peace that I receive in your Presence that I need for you to Restore.

Refresh me Oh Lord

Ways to be refreshed Spiritually can look like

- Meditating on God's Word... His Goodness, His Blessings, Healing, and Miracles in your life as well as His Provision and Love for you...

  - Praise is a powerful way to be refreshed in the presence of God. Praise is a response to the goodness of God when you recognize it.

  - Be free. Your praise doesn't need to look like anyone else's.

  - Be authentic. Praise Him however you praise Him.

Praise helps to set your mind on the good things and to celebrate how wonderful God is. It helps you to shake off negativity, doubt, fear, and whatever is paralyzing you or has you stuck. Praise also creates and cultivates internal joy that is not predicated on what is going on externally. So, what I'm saying is that if things aren't going well at work or home or with a friend or even in your body, praise changes things on the inside. When you think about how much God loves you and that there is NOTHING too hard for Him. That thought cultivates joy on the inside that fills you up and overflows in spite of the things that don't seem to be working in your favor on the outside of you. We all need that!

PRAYER

Breath Prayers.

- This is a way that we can take deep breaths and then pray short one sentence prayers that are strengthening like:

- I don't know what to do, but Lord, my eyes are on YOU.

- I feel so weak right now, but Father, I know that your strength is made perfect in weakness.

- I need you Lord and I know that you are a very present help in a time of trouble.

Praying without ceasing.

- Praying like this sounds daunting but it simply means being open and apt to pray and to hear from God anytime, anywhere. This happens by opening your heart, your ears and your eyes to feel God, sense Him, and see Him moving throughout your day.

- Praying without ceasing also helps you to become more sensitive to God's presence allowing you to better recognize His promptings, which helps you to be quicker in obeying His nudges.

Connecting with your Inner Circle of people who will pray with and for you.

- This is you're your group of faith filled people who love you and love God. They pray with you, and they pray for you. They are like-minded people. These are people who will believe with you for your healing. These are people who will not allow you to give up no matter how difficult things get. These are the people who will fight with you in prayer and with their faith fueling words.

Embracing your faith Community.

- This is the place where you come together with your family of believers. This is where your faith can be fueled together with others. A place where you can lock arms with other sisters and brothers in the body of Christ to do life together. Get to know them, love them and pray for them as sisters and brothers. You worship together, support one another and make an impact in the community for Christ.

Grow with Grace...

- **Enjoy every moment you spend in the presence of God, and you'll spend more moments in His presence.** Don't be legalistic or go by what someone says that you're supposed to do. This is your relationship with your Father, your Creator, the ONE who loves you deeply. You are the one who cultivates and nurtures that relationship to be everything that you desire for it to be.

Embracing Godfidence

- This is having confidence in the God inside of you. Having confidence in the God who dwells on the inside of you gives you the courage to stand up and to stand out in a world that needs to hear and to see the Christian life lived out loud. Confidence in the God in you says that you don't have to show up in this world pretending to be perfect BUT you can be authentically YOU and still be loved immensely by God, flaws and all. Godfidence is the confidence in God that says "I'm going to get out there and Boldly live my life, Loving God with all of my heart and love people with all that I got, Gods way.

Godfidence is trusting that He who has begun a good work in you will continue it until Jesus returns.

And I am certain that God, who began the good work within you, will continue his work until it is finally finished on the day when Christ Jesus returns.

Philippians 1:6

I want to leave this note for you if you are not a spiritual person. You can implement all of the things taught within this book and experience radical change in your life BUT to do these things without opening your heart to God and allowing Him to heal you from the inside out will only bring about temporary change.

God is the ONLY source of TRUE Healing. He loves you and wants to be in a relationship with you. He knows everything about you, and He still loves you and chooses you. God knows your story and he cares. He loves you and has a plan for your healing. Using the techniques shared in this book are really a blessing and will help you but I want you to know that God has a divine plan to heal you in ways that you could never have imagined.

With all of the things that we have discussed in this chapter, I need for you to understand that by deciding to prioritize a life of self-care you will experience radical growth and healing in your life. You won't regret it! We talked about Relational wellness goal ideas, Emotional wellness goal ideas, Physical wellness goal ideas and Spiritual wellness goal ideas. Grab a hold of these things and run with the things that work for you. Approach these things with an open mind. Try being open to expressing yourself in new ways and trying new things. I'm sure you will find many things that you will really enjoy!

Chapter Eleven:

PRIORITIZING YOUR WELLBEING

Prioritizing your wellbeing is foundational
to loving yourself well; empowering you
to face life's challenges with resilience.

LOVING YOURSELF WELL

All in all, the most important and consequential thing in all that we've discussed is how important it is for you to love yourself well by taking good care of yourself, especially during difficult times. I shared some ideas of ways that you can get started but I'm going to tell you right now that you gotta just begin. Don't allow little things to hold you back from beginning your self-care journey. This is your life, your wellbeing, your healing, and your journey. You don't need to start perfectly BUT you do need to start.

Take the reigns of your life and begin to guide yourself towards the healing that you've been waiting for. I know that your life is busy. I know that you have people and things to take care of BUT I promise you this. All of the things that you have to do will be done so much better when you decide to prioritize taking care of yourself.

Oh yes, I take this seriously. I believe that God called me to ignite the passion in people to live life loving themselves and others well, especially through difficult times. Knowing that this is my assignment, I have to take good care of myself.

If I'm not well, I won't be able to walk alongside you to support you and love you well and that's a NO for me! I love myself and I love you too. I had to make the decision to fight for my wellbeing and I still have to consciously choose to make that decision every day. Some days I do well and some days I don't, but guess what? The days I don't are far less than the days that I do because I take this seriously. I take loving myself well seriously, and I take loving you well seriously. I want you to make yourself a priority so that you will be well, while you live your life with passion and purpose.

You can do all things through Christ who
strengthens you...Philippians 4:13

DEVELOPING A SELF-CARE PLAN

I'm going to assist you in creating your very own strategically personalized self-care plan. First, you want to think about and create your Vision for your Relational, Emotional, Physical and Spiritual areas of wellness.

Vision For My Relational Wellness

_____

_____

_____

_____

Vision for My Emotional Wellness

_____

_____

_____

_____

Vision for My Physical Wellness

_____

_____

_____

_____

Vision for my Spiritual Wellness

_____

_____

_____

_____

Next, you want to envision how you want to carry out your vision. *What's the plan? How will you achieve the vision that you have?* This is setting you Macro plan to reach your vision by using the triple H method, your Head, Heart and Hands. Let me explain.

HEAD...

How do I think I can fulfill this vision? What are the things that will get in the way of me doing what I desire to do? How can I overcome, avoid or quickly recover from these things?

HEART...

How will I feel fulfilling this vision? Why is this important to me? How can I keep myself excited and motivated about doing these things?

HANDS...

This is all about doing the things you're thinking about doing to fulfill your vision. This is where you put your plans into practice. Putting pen to paper. Mapping things out. This is where you develop your micro plan using SMART goals. Your plans need to be Specific, Measurable, Achievable, Relevant and Timebound. This is what helps you to become clearer on how to implement the vision that you've expressed. If you don't plan it, it won't happen.

Specific: What exactly are you doing? (going for a walk?)

Measurable: When? Where? How? How often? How will I track this?

Achievable: Is this possible for me to achieve right now? What are my obstacles? What/who do I need to make this work?

Relevant: Is this right for me? Is this in alignment with my personal values? Will this represent me well?

Timebound: When? What day? What time?

I hope this is getting fun for you. If you're anything like me, you might be feeling excited while also feeling a little pressured. It's okay. That's the feeling that comes with making a decision. It's the pressure that you feel when you draw a line in the sand and say, 'This is what I'm going to do for me. I need this in my life, and I've made the decision to choose me!"

I know, It's a Big Deal. You're doing something special for yourself and you're not used to doing that but it's a good thing and it's cause for a celebration! Congratulations on choosing you!

I want to encourage you as you begin making changes to your life to try making changes incrementally and not by doing a complete overhaul. Changing things incrementally will drastically increase your rate of success.

Another thing that is beneficial to cementing new habits is to celebrate every win as you are putting new things into practice. Every time you do the thing you plan to do smile, clap for yourself, fist pump, cheer etc. Doing this taps the joy center in your brain and this helps you to be more likely to do it again because of the good feeling that you created by doing so.

Close your eyes for just a moment and envision the healed, stress free, joyful person that you are becoming! I'm so happy for you!

ENJOY YOUR JOURNEY

This book has taken you on quite the journey and I hope that through it you have gained some wonderful insights about yourself and how to proceed on your journey towards healing.

We talked about how your perspective colors the way that you see and experience your life and has the potential to change everything. We also talked about how the Stress, Loss Pain and Pressures of life play a huge role in the way that you define who you are; BUT you now know that you need to rethink and re-write the stories that you have been telling yourself to highlight your strength through your struggles. You now understand that doing so helps you to see your victories and triumphs through adversity.

We took time to look at your relationships but didn't stop there, you did the hard work of looking inward to see yourself, to hear yourself and to find yourself. You learned how important it is to prioritize your wellbeing and now have a roadmap to creating your very own strategically personalized self-care plan. There's no stopping you now!

EACH ONE TEACH ONE

There are so many people who need to hear this message of help, hope and healing. Take what you've learned and share it with your friends and family. Teach it to your children. Start a small group in your church, in your school or at your job. You have the power to impact the world around you. I'm so honored that you trusted me to go on this journey with you. Blessings to You!

REFERENCES

Author Unknown. (01/23/19) Vital Signs. Cleveland Clinic. Retrieved from, (https://my.clevelandclinic.org/health/articles/10881-vital-signs)

Coffee, D. (2014). The 7 Most Important Relationships. Mankato, MN: Total Person Publishing

Trimm, C. (2015). Prevail: Discover your Strength in Hard Places. Shippensburg, PA: Destiny Images Publishers Inc

ABOUT THE AUTHOR

Priscilla Coffee is an emotional wellness counselor and coach. She has a Masters in Pastoral Counseling Crisis Response & Trauma from Liberty University. She has been a hospital chaplain, pastoral counselor, crisis counselor, coach and caregiver in some capacity for her entire working career. Priscilla knows what it means to be so busy focusing on the day to day and caring for others that looking to your own needs is an afterthought that is often missed entirely. Priscilla also knows that continuing in this way is a recipe for disaster. There is a better way. Just Breathe unveils how the rhythm of breathing through life's difficulties allows you to live life loving yourself and others well, especially through difficult times. You have this book in your hand because you need it for yourself or for someone you love. There's a message of healing within these pages that was written just for you. Open it. Read it. Let your healing journey begin!

9 798218 329624